Dynamising Liberation Movements in Southern Africa: Quo Vadis?

Editors

Kgothatso Shai and Siphamandla Zondi

ISBN: 978-0-620-85121-3

Published by Ziable Publisher in partnership with IPAD

Typesetting, book layout and design by Bono Multimedia

Book Cover design by Brand Cupid World

Contents

Acknowledgements

Individual authors would like to record particular appreciation to the following journals who accepted the testing of the raw research ideas that laid a solid foundation for the earlier drafts of some of the chapters included in this book: *African Renaissance, Journal of Economics and Behavioral Studies, Journal of Public Affairs, and Ubuntu: Journal of Conflict and Social Transformation.*

We are also indebted to the National Institute of Humanities and Social Sciences (NIHSS) which generously and to a particular extent, sponsored this book project by injecting a seed funding in favour of the South African Association of Political Studies - Limpopo Chapter (SAAPS-LC) during the year 2017/8. This book represents one among the many achieved measurable outputs for this sponsorship.

LIST OF CONTRIBUTORS

Emeka A Ndaguba is a Research Assistant at the Department of Public Administration, University of Fort Hare and researcher in Governance, North-West University.

Josephat Mutangadura is a Senior Lecturer in Applied Languages at Tshwane University of Technology, South Africa.

Katija B Khan is Professor of Media Studies at the University of South Africa (UNISA).

Kgothatso B Shai is an Associate Professor and Head of Department of Cultural and Political Studies at the University of Limpopo, South Africa.

Makhura B Rapanyane is a Masters candidate in International Politics at the University of Limpopo, South Africa.

Olusola Ogunnubi is a Research Fellow at Mangosuthu University of Technology (MUT), South Africa.

Sehlare Makgetlaneng is the Executive Director of the Institute for Preservation and Development (IPAD), South Africa.

Siphamandla Zondi is Professor of Political Sciences at the University of Pretoria, South Africa.

Chapter One

Setting the scene for dynamising liberation movements in Southern Africa: *Quo Vadis*?

Kgothatso Shai and Siphamandla Zondi

Background

It is with great honour and privilege for having served as the co-editors of this book volume. In the next pages, we present a few of our shared thoughts about some of the pertinent issues relating to liberation movements in Southern Africa. Our wish was to have had a prologue of this book written by one of the elders of the liberation struggle in South[ern] Africa. Due to the reasons that are beyond our control, we found ourselves in a difficult situation of having to proceed with the production of this book without an envisaged contribution by one of the veterans of the liberation struggle in South[ern] Africa. Despite this setback, this introductory chapter has benefited a lot from the thought-provoking conversation between comrade George Mashamba and Prof Kgothatso Shai during August 2019 in Polokwane.

The elders' input on such an ambitious book project is particularly important. This is because we live in a society wherein the Westernised knowledge hegemony has brainwashed us to believe that regardless of their knowledge, activism and energy, elders are naturally isolated and dejected from active academic and policy discourses. This is the greatest weakness about Africa; which cannot be observed in Europe and North America. Our indictment of this premise dovetails with the English adage which says that "whisky matures with age". So, the conversation referred to above has exposed us to a critical and rare knowledge on the past and present history of the politics of liberation in South[ern] Africa. Unlike the contributors of the individual chapters and editors of this book, Mashamba hesitantly shared his reservoir of knowledge even though he does not believe that he is "well-learned". This should be understood within the context that he spent ten years at Robben Island prison. While in prison, he was not lucky to receive financial study support due to reasons that are beyond the scope of this chapter and book as a whole. As such, his thoughts about the cause, context and evolution of liberation movements has been largely influenced by his painful personal experience of the struggle and encounters with freedom fighters from elsewhere in South[ern] Africa, particularly from Zimbabwe and Namibia. While in prison, he had the privilege of serving as the ANC head of political education and, as such, he did self-teaching exercises by reading the political, especially communist literature.

Written from a South[ern] angled lens by contributors who belong to different generations of the witnesses of the dynamisation of the liberation movements in Southern Africa, this book is intellectually stimulating and timely. While the arguments advanced in individual chapters are not necessarily in harmony, there is no question about the coherence of the chapters entailed in this book. As such, it inspires confidence that most of the analysis and documentation represented by this book about African liberation movements was done by Africans and for Africans. While the book is relevant, we should hasten to point out that we do not necessarily agree with all the arguments advanced. Such reservation is borne of our perspectives as we fully understand that scholarship is the contestation of ideas. We might have certain reservations about the traditions and doctrines that birthed what is known as academic freedom; but we have a healthy respect for this fundamental freedom that is cherished in the Constitution of the democratic South Africa. Hence, in real life situations we do not have an absolute truth.

Depending on our epistemic and ontological location, grounding and orientation, what we have is the idea of truth- which is the product of a perception. Collectively, we are extremely worried about the Westernised dominant narrative that has been embraced by most academics, media and some activists about the so called "sins of incumbency" on the part of the liberation movements in Southern Africa and Africa as a whole. Our conviction is that this is a fallacy. Liberation movements such as the ANC do not suffer from the sins of incumbency. Incumbency presents an avalanche of opportunities for the liberation movements to exercise state power for the benefit of the people. Unfortunately, the liberation movements' deficit of thought and ethical leadership causes them to stagnate and ultimately fail to complete their historic and strategic mission. The premise for this observation is that history does not have a space for stagnation. As such, the only prospects for liberation movements are either to go backward or forward. In the post-colonial era, going forward entails confronting the inhuman and brutal system of capitalism as represented by Western hegemony. In quagmire of either standing with the Western powers or the people, the easiest route for the liberation movements is normally to stand with the former.

This should be understood within the context that most liberation movements in Southern Africa have a tendency of submitting to scare tactics of the Western powers due to the fear of being isolated by them. It is on this basis that gradually, liberation movements are losing their relevance because of the [un]conscious breakdown of the moral contract that they have previously entered with the people. Consequently, the end result is that liberation movements are regressing towards backwardness simply because they are fundamentally suffering from sins of stagnation, instead of "sins of incumbency". At this juncture, it is crucial for scholars to shift away from the individual level of analysis in pondering the liberation movements' future of the past and the past of the future. An eminent call for political scholars and practitioners is made for them to seriously reflect on strategic and tactical ideas (not individuals) on how liberation movements can be retained and used as political organs to take the struggle to another level and/ or at most, to complete the liberation cause which is still lagging in both political and economic fronts. As opposed to the popular belief that governing liberation movements have political power and not economic power; we unapologetically submit that, governing liberation movements neither have political nor economic power. In the post-colonial era (and post-apartheid era in the case of South Africa), governing liberation movements have access to political office. But real political and economic power is still in the hands of the white minority. These are the political conundrums that need to be well diagnosed in order for relevant and sustainable solutions to be conceived. "Power, to the people/ matimba, a hina"; and not liberation movements. If liberation movements mismanage power, it is the shared moral and humanitarian responsibility of the people to take their power.

Rationale

The historic Arab and European intrusion into Africa has been met with collaboration and resistance by the locals as soon as it became apparent that it was poised to destabilise the way of life of the Africans. It is evident that this intrusion later manifested itself into oppression and exploitation of the Africans. The role of the Arabs in this regard was short-lived and displaced when the partitioning of Africa among the European powers was formalised in the Berlin conference during the 18th century. It is to state the obvious to mention that colonialism in Africa was preceded by slavery. Some Africans, especially African traditional leaders were complicit to the perpetuation of the enslavement and colonisation of their nations in order to carry favours and privileges from the slave masters and colonisers. Most Africans, who are the majoritarian segment of the population in Africa and the indigenes of the same continent, individually and collectively resisted slavery and colonialism in different ways.

Such resistance also ushered the establishment of liberation movements which were to be used as the vanguards for fostering unity and solidary among the oppressed African masses within and between different countries in Africa and African diaspora. Among the liberation movements to be established include the ANC in South Africa, Zimbabwe African National Union-Patriotic Front (ZANU-PF), South West African People's Organisation (SWAPO) in Namibia, Front for the Liberation of Mozambique (FRELIMO) and People's Movement for the Liberation of Angola (MPLA). Like liberation movements in other parts of Africa, those in Southern Africa were equally instrumental in the fight and defeat of colonialism. However, this victory is mooted by some observers who argue that liberation movements in Southern Africa have only attained political freedom for the people and they are either failing or at the cross-road in terms of the realisation of economic freedom.

Despite these imperfections on the part of the liberation movements cum ruling political parties, it appeared they still carried the hopes of the majority of Africans at least until in the 21st century. Before this time, these political parties seemed to survive by punting into liberation rhetoric and solidarity among themselves. However, the political developments of the year 2017 in Zimbabwe and 2018 in South Africa show that historical imperatives are becoming fast irrelevant in defining the content and direction of modern politics in Southern Africa. The commonalities in trends and patterns in terms of how Robert Mugabe and Jacob Zuma were forced out of their respective positions led some commentators to conclude that these events signify the "Black Spring", the Southern Africa version of Arab Spring. This should be understood within the context of the unique position of this region and the potential of political developments in South Africa and Zimbabwe to have spill over effects towards these countries' neighbours due to the former's political and geographical status in Southern Africa.

The discourse on this subject is highly polarised because of the competing interests of local and international actors who are affected by key political developments in Southern Africa in one way or the other. It is worth emphasising that accounts in this regard are fragmented and most of the time, are among scholars from one academic discipline (i.e. Political Science). This tendency among scholars to operate in silos or within their disciplinarian boundaries causes the existing body of knowledge to miss valuable perspectives that could be generated from other disciplines in a form of book projects that assumes an interdisciplinary, multidisciplinary and transdisciplinary posture. Adding to the bipolarity of this discourse, dynamism in terms of the place and role of liberation movements which are in government within Southern Africa is poised to make them potentially rich avenues for on-going research by political thinkers emanating from political science, public affairs, sociology, media studies and other cognitive disciplines. However, what emerges from the existing literature on this subject is that most studies on this subject are conducted from a North[ern] angled perspective.

The questions we ask in this book are: (i) Does the idea of 'liberation' still has a place in Southern Africa? (ii) With the several changes in leadership sweeping across the region, are we seeing a new brand of politics that diametrically resists or contests liberation ideals? (iii) Can the future of liberation movements be predicted? (iv) Can these movements be renewed?

Statement of purpose

Based on a select of test cases, the primary aim of this interdisciplinary book is to take stock of the state of liberation movements in Southern Africa. This aim is informed by the fact that the study of the reconciliation of the past and present politics of liberation movements can never be complete without a rigorous and systematic focus on Southern Africa and through the South[ern] angled lens. The aim of this book will be achieved by delving into the following objectives:

- Analyse the transition of liberation movements into governing parties
- Identify and tease out the common challenges and key issues plaguing

liberation movements' incumbency

- Forecast the future of liberation solidarity in Southern Africa

- Showcase refreshing perspectives on the journey travelled thus far by the liberation movements

- Compare and contrast the performance of liberation movements led governments in Southern Africa

- Describe the patterns and trends of practice by Southern Africa's liberation movements

The practical public policy purpose and content of this book project

The purpose of this book project is not purely an academic one. Its purpose serves a task specified by public policy or political practice as policy makers of the Southern African countries confront or face current situation in their internal and external relations. All contributors of its chapters are scholars. Scholars are intellectual workers engaged in the production of knowledge vital to the development of their countries. They constantly remind policy makers of their countries in particular that they should not be hostile to the development of theoretical positions especially on the governing political parties as required by the present situation. This is of vital and special importance given the fact that governing political parties provide their societies with official direction in their internal and external relations. It is for this reasons that this book project is important in contributing towards the concrete understanding of the state of affairs of Southern Africa's governing political parties.

As an intellectual project of practical public policy purpose and content, this book project subscribes to the thesis of the unity of theory and practice. Central to this thesis is that theory emerges out of practice and in turn serves practice. Very often the importance of executing the intellectual task of developing theoretical positions to take care of the practical requirements of the current situation is opposed in the name of defending established theoretical positions. What is the purpose of defending established theoretical positions on the governing political parties and their leaders in the Southern African countries, if they are incapable of adequately appropriating the political governance of their societies and their performance on the critical areas of human rights, democracy, development as far as the satisfaction of the interests, needs and demands of the people of their countries are concerned in their current situation?

This book project serves the Southern African societies as they confront and face their current socio-political and economic problems under the leadership of their governing political parties which served as their national liberation movements. Most importantly, it serves South Africa as the regional power in the Southern African region. This is of vital importance for various reasons. South Africa has been using its own enormous human and financial resources in its contributions towards the resolution of problems in countries such as the

Democratic Republic of Congo, Lesotho, Zimbabwe and those beyond the region. As a member state of the Southern African Development Community (SADC), it has been shouldering responsibility at the request of the regional body in the efforts of resolving conflicts in some of the regional countries and contributing towards the sustenance of SADC as the regional economic community. This is important given that this is the means through which Southern Africa contributes not only towards its regional integration but more importantly, African continental integration. As a member of the Southern African Customs Union (SACU), it has been playing a leadership role in contributing towards the national budget and development of Botswana, Lesotho, Namibia and Swaziland as its customs union partners. There is a high level of nationals of Southern Africa and of other countries of the African continent in the South Africa for various reasons. South Africa through its administrative capital, Pretoria is the second to Washington D.C. as the host of embassies and high commissions in the world. This is the reflection of the global strategic importance of our country.

Given this reality, there is a higher level of expectations placed upon South Africa regionally, continentally and globally for it to increase its leadership role in African affairs in the interest of the people of the Southern African region and the African continent and to contribute towards a better world. It is for these reasons, among others, that the book project is of vital importance for South Africa in its role in African and global affairs and for its own popular national interests.

Organisation of the book project

In terms of chapter breakdown, this book is made up of ten chapters including this introductory chapter by the editors. Thereafter, Siphamandla Zondi lays a foundation stone for this book in chapter two. On the basis of an Afrodecolonial lens Zondi shows the nexus between the idea of liberation movements, liberation struggle and the transition to independence and democracy in order to respond to the call for movements to become parties. In this regard, the central question that Zondi grapples with in this chapter is: Should Movements Transition into Political Parties? Moving from popular and Western rooted narrative, Zondi makes a strong case that there is no real value to be derived from transitioning liberation movements into political parties for what is needed is to decolonise the state by fundamentally transforming the inherited political, economic and social systems, and renegotiating the agency of African state in the neoliberal neo-colonial world system. In the absence of the decolonisation of the state, the morphing of liberation movements into modern political parties would not necessarily produce a political playfield wherein democratic and/or competitive politics can thrive.

Flowing from the above, chapter three by Kgothatso Shai and Olusola Ogunnubi reminds us that for more than two decades, 21st March has been canonised and celebrated among South Africans as Human Rights Day. Earmarked by the newly democratic and inclusive South Africa, it commemorates the Sharpeville and Langa massacres. As history recorded, on the 21st March 1960, residents of Sharpeville and subsequently, Langa embarked on a peaceful anti-pass campaign led by the ANC breakaway party, the Pan Africanist Congress of Azania (PAC). The pass (also known as *dompas*) was one of the most despised symbols of apartheid; a system declared internationally as a crime against humanity. In the post-apartheid era, it is expected that all South Africans enjoy and celebrate the full extent of their human rights.

However, Shai and Ogunnubi suggest that the envisaged rights are not equally enjoyed by all. This is because widening inequalities in the health-care system, in schooling, and in the lucrative sporting arena have not been amicably and irrevocably resolved. Furthermore, it is still the norm that the most vulnerable of South Africans, especially rural Africans, find it difficult, and sometimes, impossible to access adequate and even essential healthcare services. Central to the possible questions to emerge from this discourse are the following (i) What is the current state of South Africa's health system at the turn of second decade of its majority rule? (ii) Why is the South African health system still unable to sufficiently deliver the socioeconomic health rights of most South African people? It is against this background that this chapter provides a nuanced Afrocentric assessment of South Africa's human rights record in the health sector since the year 1994.

In chapter four, Kgothatso Shai and Emeka Ndaguba submit that if the ANC is to evade the wrath of coalition politics in the near future; it needs more than its traditional support base and appeals for liberation rhetoric. Like other liberation movements *cum* ruling political parties in Southern Africa, indications are that ANC cannot save itself from the brutality of competitive politics and electoral democracy. While the ANC is based in South Africa, it remains the political heritage of all Africans and as such, it can only survive further degeneration through the collective efforts of Pan-Africanists in the country and across the corners of the continent. The fact that President Jacob Zuma-led ANC did not have a safe liberalised space for counsel by non-active members has rendered any possible renewal through the support of all Africans a pipe-dream.

While the renewal of the ANC may be necessary for the sake of preserving liberation heritage in South Africa and Africa at large; it is concluded by Shai and Ndaguba that the weakening of dominant political parties such as the ANC is a necessary ingredient for healthy and functioning democracies. This observation should be understood within the context that no political party and/or liberation movement is entitled to state power. State power belongs to the people and therefore, at no stage should any political organ be viewed as being more than the people. Hence, political parties (especially liberation movements) are the products of the struggles of the people. They are established by the people. It is not political parties that created the people and their respective struggles. It is on this basis that as and when liberation movements and political parties in general, loses touch with the people, they are bound to crumple as it is currently the case with the ANC and ZANU-PF, just to mention a few.

In chapter five, Sehlare Makgetlaneng draws from the insights of ANC's diverse membership for the purpose of identifying and locating three key challenges faced by the movement in its exercise of state power. What clearly emerges from this chapter is that ANC is popularly viewed as the proud national product produced by South Africans in their struggle to end their socio-historical injustice. It became in this process, producer of activities aimed at earning and sustaining respect, trust and loyalty of the South African people so as to organise effectively for socio-political and economic change. It produced unassailable quality of leadership and general membership who through risks, courageous acts and principled lives enabled it in moving theory and analysis to practice through mobilisation and concrete action that led to its victory over the forces of the apartheid rule in 1994. However, the ANC is currently facing profound unprecedented challenges in its history as a governing party. With Jacob Zuma's accession to the national presidency and an assailable quality of his administration and their consequences, its members increasingly recognised and admitted this reality. Rather than decreasing as a result of Cyril Ramaphosa becoming its president and that of the country, these challenges have continued increasing. What led to these challenges?

The first reasons provided by some ANC members attribute challenges it is facing to Thabo Mbeki, others maintain that Jacob Zuma was responsible for them. Their agreement is that it was under their respective leadership that the movement lost its historical direction or way. The second view attributes its challenges to its historical neglect of economic and social thinking in its political strategy since its formation in 1912. The consequence is that this negatively affected the quality and creativity of its policy thinking in the turning point of the history of the movement towards post-apartheid era. Its decisive impact on the content of the transition and its economic policy options and choices led to its assailable performance in dealing with socio-economic and corruption problems and governance and development challenges.

The third view attributes its challenges to its shortcomings and mistakes it made in exile. According to this reasoning, the movement did not seriously discuss the South African economy and its relation to global capitalism. Rather, the ANC was only ready to negotiate, not to govern. Its readiness to negotiate was 'punctuated by conspicuous shortcomings.' It had no serious policy to build a new society. The consequence is that it was vulnerable from the first day it served as a governing party. It has no reliable policy in almost strategic areas, including concrete plans for uniting South Africans to a common cause. Its national policy conferences since its unbanning were inadequate in providing it with reliable policies that would have enabled it to govern South Africa effectively, efficiently, responsibly and progressively. As a means of contributing towards the concrete understanding of the ANC challenges and their sources, the chapter thus focuses its attention on their views by the ANC members through the journey it has travelled thus far in facing challenges and key issues of which it is both producer and product.

In chapter six, Kgothatso Shai analyses the state of then Jacob Zuma-led ANC as a liberation movement *cum* ruling political party of South Africa. In particular, he employs Afrocentricity as an alternative contextual lens to identify and tease out the perceived major contradictions that characterised the Zuma-led ANC. The central question grappled with in this chapter is: to determine whether the political and ideological contradictions as displayed by the differing views of the prominent ANC-led tripartite alliance represents the emergence or continuity of the real or imagined contradictions in the governing ANC? It is argued in this chapter that the major contradictions espoused by the leadership of the ANC can best be understood when located within historicity and the context of the elective national conference of the party that was held in December 2017. Even though this chapter's historical sensibility forces it to briefly reflect on some of the key historical imperatives before the year 2009, its analysis is located within the Zuma's ANC/South African presidency.

In a dialogue with Sahm Venter's *Conversations with a Gentle Soul,* Kgothatso Shai uses the chapter seven of this book to reflect on the X-ray of Ahmed Kathrada to weigh on the meaning and essence of some of the theology imbued political opinions of selected national leaders of the ANC. Overall, the fundamental question addressed here is: what are the [dis]continuities of the religious virtue[s] of the ANC since its transition from a liberation movement to governing party during the year 1994? This chapter argues that in the main, the current crop of ANC leaders is not individually and collectively committed to the fundamental principles of the party's theology. In fact, they [ab]use theological expressions to achieve short-term political party goals.

In chapter eight Makhura Rapanyane analyses the realities of the ANC's hegemonic shrink in the Jacob Zuma and Cyril Ramaphosa's administrations (incumbent) using their terms of office in the form of periodization approach. The principal objective of this chapter is to highlight the significant hegemonic detractors in the last decade and possible more, if not attended to, in the coming five years of Ramaphosa's first-term in office. Equally important, this chapter centrally concludes that the ANC is slowly but surely losing power.

Katija Khan places the discourse on the arrogance of "entitlement" to sustain liberation political parties' hold onto power in Southern Africa within a historical context. In chapter nine she argues that the period stretching between the 1930s to the late 1990 saw many Southern African countries engage in decisive liberation wars to reclaim their independence from colonial governments. The earliest countries to attain independence in Southern Africa were Zambia and Mozambique, the latest being Namibia and South Africa. Zimbabwe's independence came in 1980 after a negotiated settlement brokered by Britain at the Lancaster Conference in 1979. The official installation of majority rule in South Africa during the year 1994 has heralded Southern Africa's total transition from colonial rule to the nationalistic liberation movements led democratic dispensation. The possession of war credentials saw these liberation heroes and movements claiming lifetime entitlement to leadership and endless access to resources. The implication was that once the liberation movement had vanquished colonialism, history would dictate that it should (or would) stay in power forever. R. W. Johnson (2001) clarifies this when he writes of national liberation movements (NLMs) as sharing a "common theology".

Josephat Mutangadura closes this book by highlighting that the history of mass media emanated from man's struggle for liberty and freedom, which include freedom of expression, and the freedom to express oneself. This struggle was started in the years around the 1700. It is from this era that enriched politicians started investing greatly in setting up the media industry, in order to reach-out to their exclusive target audience. The media is an instrumental tool that has both good and bad results. In particular, this chapter intended to trace and analyse how the ZANU-PF government has been using the public media, specifically print newspapers and electronic media as mouthpieces to sell its propaganda stories. The ruling party has been in power for close to forty years now and the population has grown dissatisfied with its policies which continue to impoverish the people. The government failing is now being blamed on external forces' interference with the work of the ruling party, and in support of the opposition. The specific script being sold to the people, both internal and external, is that, Western powers have imposed sanctions on the country in an attempt to force for regime change in the country.

The government of ZANU-PF engaged in a number of failed policies and in the end, analysts began to view all these attempts as a planned effort to enrich the government officials through policies that were not pro-people, but the ruling part in the name of liberators. When the situation in the country became dire, the opposition started making inroads as shown through election results, and the ruling part started a spirited campaign through government-controlled media to recolonize the people's mind through propaganda material. The chapter, thus focused on, biased reporting, opinion columns, commentaries and cartoon strips developed with the agenda to force a mindset change in the electorate that seem to be departing from the age-old belief that liberation parties have peoples' concern at heart.

Chapter Two

Liberation movements and modern democracy: Should movements transition into political parties?

Siphamandla Zondi

Introduction

The argument for the transition of liberation movements is different from one of reform because it is about them taking on a new form and nature on the basis that the new environment needed something different from what they are. The argument is generally that liberation movements were part of the necessary social and political machinery for fighting an imposed system of colonialism, including apartheid. In their ideological outlook, their political culture, their institutional make-up and their policy agenda, they were fit for that purpose, namely to end colonialism and usher in a post-colonial era. The reasoning is that with the fall of colonialism (Namibia) and apartheid (South Africa) in the 1990s such a condition that required liberation movements ended and a new era of competitive political party democracy had been ushered in. The argument is that either liberation movements morph into modern political parties or they will become a major reason for the failure of postcolonial democracy. To illustrate this, critics point to the phenomenon they call party dominance, stifling the growth of a multiparty system as a necessary feature of modern democracy.

This argument has been made repeatedly in reference to southern African countries where liberation movements have remained in charge of six countries (Angola, Mozambique, Namibia, Tanzania, South Africa and Zimbabwe). This chapter reflects on the basis of an Afrodecolonial lens on the idea of liberation movements, liberation struggle and the transition to independence and democracy in order to respond to the call for movements to become parties. To do this, it begins with a short outline of our lens of analysis in the belief that without a clear understand of the analytical lens the argument may not make sense. We will conclude with an argument in response to the transition to party call.

Afrodecolonial lens of analysis

Since we intend to enter into a structured debate with the voices that have argued for the end of liberation movements and a birth of political parties in southern Africa, we need an epistemic lens that will enable us to understand liberation movements and the reasons for their endurance well beyond independence to the chagrin of those who believe their *raison d'etre* ceases at independence. We need an analytical framework that would explain fundamental dynamics that underpin these political institutions, their conduct, their ideological content, their political projects and their conduct in and out of power. The idea of a free-floating signifier who observes things from a somewhat neutral point of view, holding to an objective observation of phenomena, is rejected outright as incapable of helping one navigate through a contested terrain. It is also a myth that Eurocentrism has sold to the world as it championed rationality as a prism of thought, as it has been shown several times.

Subaltern scholars including black, black feminist, Chicana, critical scholars from the South, revolutionary African thinkers and others have shown that all speak from particular locations even if they are speaking into the whole world or speaking with other worlds. No one should claim the privilege of speaking from nowhere or from everywhere, because such is to arrogate to themselves the power to universalise their particularities at the expense of others'. "No one escapes", Ramon Grosfoguel (2009: 13) argues, "the class, sexual, gender, spiritual, linguistic, geographical, and racial hierarchies of the 'modern/colonial capitalist/patriarchal world-system'", which is what he calls the bio-politics of knowledge manifesting in the dominance of Eurocentrism as the ego-politics of Western philosophy of knowledge. Enrique Dussel (1980) calls this the geo-politics of knowledge that find expression in the fact that all thinking is born in a particular geo-political space. "I am speaking of political space," he explained in *Philosophy of Liberation*, "which includes all existentially real spaces within the parameters of an economic system in which power is exercised in tandem with military control". For this reason, he thought of his thinking and writing as 'situated' as Molefi Asante (1987) would say of Afrocentricity. Dussel explained further to say, "I am trying, then, to take space, geopolitical space, seriously. To be born at the North Pole or in Chiapas is not the same thing as to be born in New York City"(Dussel, 1980: 2). The implications of this for those writing about the realities in political spaces such as those that straddle colonialism and independence, apartheid and neo-apartheid democracy, liberation struggle and rainbow nation are eloquently explained in this the following quote:

> *Distant thinkers, those who had a perspective of the center from the periphery, those who had to define themselves in the presence of an already established image of the human person and in the presence of uncivilized fellow humans, the newcomers, the ones who hope because they are always outside, these are the ones who have a clear mind for pondering reality. They have nothing to hide. How could they hide domination if they undergo it? How would their philosophy be an ideological ontology if their praxis is one of liberation from the center they are opposing? Philosophical intelligence is never so truthful, clean, and precise as when it starts from oppression and does not have to defend any privileges, because it has none (ibid, 4).*

For these reasons, the centres and margins that emerged as a result of the global colonial enterprise and its Cartesian epistemic enterprise become important political and epistemic locations that impinge on what is said, what is understood and how things are thought through. Power in political, economic, cultural and epistemic forms has its geography, as Richard Pit shows, resulting in "the concentration of power in a few spaces that control a world of distant others"(Peet, 2007: 4). This makes the locus of enunciation, the geopolitical, ideological, epistemic space from one speaks an important element of my speaking, especially because we are speaking from the periphery where we have nothing, have nothing therefore to hide. This is sharp contrast to Eurocentrism.

> *By delinking ethnic/racial/gender/sexual epistemic location from the subject that speaks, western philosophy and sciences are able to produce a myth about a Truthful <u>Universal knowledge</u> that conceals who is speaking, as well as, obscuring the geo-political and body-political epistemic location in the structures of colonial power/knowledge from which the subject speaks* (Grosfoguel, 2009: 14)

The implications of this has been to distort the diverse nature of knowledge by forcing the thinkers from the South to mimic those of the North who pretend not to come from this particular location, but to be objective knowledge workers pursuing universal interests. Being from and being committed to the centre, they have a lot to hide; they have atrocities, genocides, epistemicides, valuecides and linguicides, and the muzzling of the voices of the other to hide. They have a whole culpability of Eurocentrism and complicity of Western science in the imperial and colonial projects with all their violence and injustice. It is difficult to admit that they think from within the unjust system of power, being and knowing, so they have to create a fictitious location called objective, a God's eye view, to hide their culpability in.

As Dussel says, there is absolutely no reason why philosophers of liberation, thinkers from the margins, writers from the periphery, voices from the underside of Euromodernity, scholars from the belligerent South should replicate the Eurocentric position, for they have completely nothing to hide. For as Archie Mafeje (2011) has argued, the idea of a free-floating signifier ensconced in the objective epistemic position is a myth for the simple reason that for us thinkers and voices speaking from the periphery of the geopolitics of knowledge, we speak in response to realities in our spaces. The issues we deal with arise significantly from the encroachment upon this space. So, we write in response to negations replete in the dominant discourse, distortions that disfigure the realities of the world we come from. We have entered the terrain of epistemic liberation from what Paulin Hountondji calls extraversion by which we export Southern data in order to import Western paradigms, theory and assumptions (Hountondji, 1997) so we can take the position Asante illustrate in the questions: "So that it becomes legitimate to ask, 'Where is the sistah coming from?' or 'Where is the brotha at?' 'Are you down with overcoming oppression?' "(Asante, 2009: 3).

This response to a mainstream discourse about liberation movements and the postcolony is framed by decolonial thought as a philosophy of liberation with African specificities, what we call Afrodecolonial lens. Decolonial thought is a diverse planet-wide school of thought that emerged on the peripheries as thinkers at the margins of a neo-colonial world engaged in negating the negations of the imposed global centre. It takes seriously the continuities between colonial and postcolonial moments, manifesting in the coloniality of being, of power and of knowledge. It is committed to shifting the geography of reason by which the excluded, muted, silenced, ignored, distorted, questioned, condemned and marginalised speak out of obscurity, unmasking the technologies of their peripheralization, rising up against exteriority and wedging a space for themselves to speak authentically from their chosen loci of enunciation and geopolitical spaces. This is a lens that makes it acceptable to disrupt the Eurocentric injustice, distortions and illusions in order to make possible truly diverse ways of knowing and grappling with realities people on the margins contend with.

Africanity as a specific occasion in this shifting geography of reasons enables negation of negations, a combative ontology, a process of claiming the African renaissance because extraverted discourses work to steal, kill and destroy the African story. It includes the Afrocentric commitment to scholarship that is situated in African view of history and its cultural implications. It includes a variety of other African perspectives committed not to merely valorising everything African, but to re-centering Africa in the story about Africa as an act of justice against prior injustice (Zeleza, 2013). All of them are joined together by a commitment to reverse the dis-memberment that left the idea of Africa not only divided by artificial geographical borders, but also fragmented by geopolitical, ideological, imposed cultural, linguistic, and theoretical worldviews and incarcerated in dependency on Euro-American world for meaning, for lenses of seeing the world, for economic and political systems of prosperity, for theories and ideologies of its struggles, for the affirmation of its humanity (Wa Thiong'o, 2009).

Together these permutations of the philosophy of liberation as a prism of thought and action give rise to what we call Afrodecolonial lens, a decolonial lens with significant input from Africanity. This study's interpretation of the mainstream debate on the need for liberation movements to transition into political parties, on the implied meanings of the post-apartheid and the post-colonial, on the meaning of political parties versus liberation movements derives from the philosophy of liberation as it relates to what it suggests we must do when we respond to mainstream discourses and designs. For instance, what purports to be objective discussions about changed political conditions in southern Africa was informed by scholarly inquiry about what was intellectually interesting in this region. Scholarship arises out of the specific life world and particular interests of certain specific communities (I borrowed from (Mills, 1998) to formulate this point). It may turn out that issues being raised arise from parochial interests of the powerful minority in pursuit of a defeat of whatever remains of the liberation struggle. It will be shown that the discourse makes certain histories, worldviews, experiences and paradigms invisible in order to perpetuate a hegemonic perspective of those who were visible under colonialism and apartheid, who want to also become ultra-visible in the post-colonial period.

The call for liberation movements to become parties

Both single-party and dominant party debates have provided the basis for arguments calling for or expecting a transition of liberation movements into political parties. This call is by no means homogenous in these debates nor is it made for the same reasons or with the same motivations. But what emerges from a careful analysis is that first, it is a widespread and growing view as assessments of liberation movements in power grow in light of governance and development crisis and secondly, the expectation of this transition is linked to assumptions about consolidation of democracy. These developments have a lot to do with the growing embrace of democracy theory as an underlying paradigm for analysing the state of politics in Africa. Therefore, to reflect on these debates we need to also understand the broad frames of the democracy debate broadly and how it is being brought onto the African scene. This is because both one-party state and dominant party debates are premised on assumptions about what democracy entails and Africa is expected to follow the pattern implied by these assumptions. I use the word assumptions advisedly to denote that these are matters of debate rather than established consensus, especially when it comes to the African region.

Democratic theory thrives in the literature and in political practice mainly because the concept of democracy - nebulous, complex and contested as it is - became dominant in the pantheon of political ideas. It is not a coherent and clearly demarcated body of knowledge. It is subject to a lot of disagreements about what is democratic theory, hence the idea that it is a loosely knit family of ideas. Even the location of this area of study is unclear with some considering it an extension of political theory, while others seeing it as an interdisciplinary endeavour drawing together political science, law, philosophy, public administration, international relations and sociology. Contestations also revolve around what is being studied, about whether it is democracy in participatory, pluralist, realist, deliberative or agonistic terms. Yet, there is a shared concern about the idea of democracy as a superior form of polity and the differences only arises when models of this democracy are discussed. Therefore, differences are on surface issues of form and character of democracy, but not on democracy itself. Since James Pennock published his book *Democratic Political Theory* in 1979 (Pennock, 1979), democratic theory debates are not really concerned about how power is managed in order to meet needs of nations and society, but how democracy is modelled. It is the presence or absence of democracy where the latter is seen as a sort of an evil, a problem and a gap to be addressed. Of course, there are democratic theorists for whom the quality of democracy is directly related to how to enable citizens to have power over the elected, but this is still really about democracy than popular power in society that could come via various political systems

Today, democracy, a particular tradition of democracy, has been made into an uncontested way to do enlightened politics and the only option among political ideas. There is no more debate about whether we need this democracy or not everywhere, but what nature and character it should take and with what effect. It has come to be that there is only one democratic theory to refer to, instead of democratic theories. This dominant democratic theory seeks to conceptualise a particular type of democracy as preferred; to frame the discussion on what is its value; to explain its promise to society especially in relation to human freedoms an institutional effectiveness and socio-economic development; and to understand counter-democratic features of modern society. In this sense, it makes sweeping observations about democracy for digestion by the whole, often on the basis of close analysis of Western nations in the belief that what obtains in the West pertains also the whole world.

Democratic theory claims that democracy "induces governments to be responsive to the preferences of the people" and political parties organize politics in modern democracy and causes it to be responsive (Stokes, 1999: 2). For this reason, parties are said to be indispensable to the practical functioning of a government and for modern representative generally. Even in recently established democracy, especially those of the so-called second and third wave of democracy, parties have acquired significant relevance and have becomes "widely seen as a sine qua non for the organisation of the modern polity and for the expression of political pluralism"(van Biezen & Katz, 2005: 2). Their role has grown both in nature and in its diversity. They are need for building and aggregating support among broad coalitions of citizens; for integrating multiple competing demands into coherent policy programs; for selecting and training politicians to play the role of legislators and executors of political programmes; for providing voters with choices of governing teams and policies; and, if elected, they are needed for organising the process of governing and accountability back to the citizens(Norris 2005; Diamond, Larry; Gunther 2001). Thus, it is thought, a democracy needs strong and sustainable political parties with the capacity to represent citizens and provide policy choices that demonstrate their ability to govern for the public good (Norris, 2005: 1). Political parties and democracy saw a renewed importance as new democracies around the globe struggle with issues of representation and governability (Stokes, 1999).

These discussions were echoed in the South generally and Africa in particular. There was a widespread embrace of democracy as an idea, especially one as conceptualised in the democratic theory (Adejumobi and Olukoshi, 2008). African scholars used terms such as the third wave of democracy, echoing the work of US-based democratic theory on the waves of democracy that connects very different experiences with political systems lumped together in a generic term, democracy. The experiences of Europe and North America in the early 19th century till 1945, which was also experienced outside Europe as a tragedy of imperialism and colonialism or as a non-democracy, are connected in this narrative with those of political changes that took place in the period after the second war that included very different experiences of political transformation as those happened in Europe's Italy and Germany for instance and those of Asian countries following colonialism. The third wave is described as the winds of changes that took place in Africa as African people stood up against Western and Soviet-backed dictatorships, bringing about more competitive political systems. This narrative enables its champions to see what they call a long period of global democratic revolution, while conceding that there were moments of reverse waves, such as the rise of fascism and nazism in the early 20th century as well as reversals in the 1962-1975 (Huntington et al., 1991). Some have referred to this as the desired rise of multiparty democracy following the violent uprisings in Algiers in 1985, followed by popular upsurge in various countries, with the effect of changing the rules of the political game and binging about meaningful reforms in the state in Africa (Nzongola-Ntalaja, 1997). Some saw in this a "surging tide of democracy" in Africa, rescuing the continent from the chains of dictatorship and authoritarianism and promising an enabling political environment for social and economic development (Chege, 1992). The achievement of liberal democracy in South Africa in 1994 thought to have completed this so-called wave led to claims that this was an African renaissance (Maloka, 2001). This discussion takes for granted that the rise of multi-partyism is in itself an expression of this wave of democracy, a desired development.

There is a whole body of literature and conversations that did not challenge the fact of this "wave", but disputed the assumption that this came from the West. African scholars have argued that at the heart of the liberation struggles was a democratic aspiration. A collection papers published at *Popular Struggles for Democracy in* Africa sought to demonstrate these grassroots and endogenous impulses behind the wave of democratisation. Written on the back of a massive authoritarian turn in Third World politics, a period the book editors call the best of time for dictators and military warlords, the book grapples with crisis of the African state as symptomatic of the crisis of the post-colony as a period and moment in Africa's long history. They argue that the crisis of democracy was in fact the diminishing role of the people in governmental affairs, the shrinking of the political area for political mobilisation in pursuit of social, political and economic justice for the downtrodden, social engineering for political demobilisation, lack of accountability and poor commitment to public interest. These deepened alongside lack of "economic democracy" manifest in the failure to transform colonial political economy, resulting in persist neo-colonial, neo-patrimonial, and comprador patterns of economic life (Nyong'o, 1987). Shivji is among those who argue that independence was merely a milestone in a long march towards democracy; it did not entail its achievement. Neither did the rise of multiparty democracy mean a beginning or the achievement of this long walk (Shivji, 2003).

But the democracy in the minds and hearts of those who mobilised in the fight against colonialism and apartheid was not liberal democracy per se, rather it was a particular kind of democracy that offers broader social liberation alongside legal rights and freedoms. It is democracy achieved when people were now able and empowered to access basic provisions like food, water and health services. In this view, what we might call the liberationist view, the struggle for democracy was a struggle for total freedom, a liberation struggle indeed. The articulation of the pursuit of democracy as a struggle for liberation, according to Shivji, "gave democracy a social dimension, which neoliberal ideology eschews and avoids"(Shivji, 2003: n.p.). The struggle had in mind popular democracy where this implies democracy from the perspective of popular classes, one with a position on imperialism, state transformation, and class interests, which distinguish it from a form of pursuit of democracy associated with western liberalism (individualism) (Saul, 1994). It is one designed to deliver social liberation rather than democratic instruments, procedures and processes that make a façade of democracy (Nzongola-Ntalaja, 1997), a realm of deferred dreams and shattered expectations (Ndlovu-Gatsheni, 2013). The view is that the struggle for genuine liberation "involves the transformation of the inherited structures of the state and the economy in order to make them capable of serving the interests of the African workers and peasants" (Nzongola-Ntalaja,1997: x).

The turn to liberal democracy is part of the mistakes of the left, which in Nyong'o's analysis consisted in the assumption that the neo-colonial state inherited could be used for a left agenda and that all that is needed to do this was to Africanise its personnel, appoint at the top men with the left language and demeanour (Nyong'o, 1987: 23). It is part of the disappointment with the evolution of democracy including how political parties have conducted themselves in power and in politics generally. This includes the take-over of political parties by a small section of political elite, the petit bourgeoisie linked to the international neoliberal industry, in the form of politicians who have mastered the game of numbers, control, manipulation and technical procedures to enable them to use parties in order to interests other that consolidating democracy, inclusion and participation. In some case they have been said to have been hijacked by mavericks, extremists and even criminal networks, thus reducing the responsiveness of governments to the citizenry as party politics become an avenue for competing interests of the elite competing over procedures and dominance of the political space.

In the 2000s, African political practitioners and analysis alike have explored if the route to this popular democracy through the building of democratic developmental states was feasible (Mkandawire, 2012). This is because of the realisation that the liberal and authoritarian routes had not worked for the continent. Neither dictatorships of the 1970s and 1980s were developmental enough to pursue social liberation nor were more liberal options tried in the 1990s and 2000s able to meet the socio-economic aspirations of the people. With the end of the Cold War in the late 1980s seen as a triumph of Western liberalism, the options had significantly narrowed. The developmental state model that assisted South-East Asian states with stronger democratic credentials became an interesting option open to Africa, one that liberation movements in southern Africa generally uneasy with Western imperialist designs explored with zest. This led to some arguing for developmental democracy based on a strong, capable, and democratic state intervening decisively in the economy in order to achieve higher levels of economic prosperity for all (Edigheji, 2005). This option is still work in progress, further encouraged by experiences of the likes of Rwanda whose developmental successes are driven by a state similar to what has been described as a developmental state with democratic credentials. The extent of these democratic credentials is a subject for debate.

Questions have been raised in democratic theory debates about the extent to which political parties have the capacity to serve the function of making the democracy responsive to the needs and interests of ordinary citizens, especially active citizens. The relationship between their objectives and organisation, on the one hand, and the demands of the democratic moment in the evolution of a country, on the other. The character of politicians and leaders responsible for running the political system as a whole, especially government have also come under a sharp scrutiny. This happens in the context of an increased disconnect between citizens and elected leaders, decline or changes in political activism, and the surge of anti-democracy and anti-establishment sentiment, taking shape in the form of political movements of various kinds. Concerns about how parties operate and function as well as about how they understand and undertake the functions seen as essential for democracy and viewed as being the responsibility of parties. Challenges of elitism worsen when problems of corruption, inefficiency and institutional weakening are add to the story (van Biezen and Katz, 2005). "More specifically," concludes Van Biezen and Katz (2005: 2), "parties are losing relevance everywhere as vehicles of representation, instruments of mobilization, and channels of interest articulation and aggregation".

As the mainstream and more established democracy have been casting a critical eye at political parties, calling into question their efficacy in the changing time, scholars in southern Africa have used the reasons as we refer to earlier in order to make the case for transition of liberation movements into political parties. These scholars have concluded that liberation movements are in inevitable decline for reasons already expressed in relation to political parties, yet part of this discussion suggests that liberation movements should transition into political parties. Political part, an idea that are seen as being in decline in Europe and North America is expected to be the answer to the decline experienced by liberation movements. Writing epistemically from the world that is growing fatigued with parties as a tool for deepening democracy, these scholars champion the establishment of new parties and strengthening the old ones in order to deepen democracy in Africa. There is a challenge right there; that institutions facing existential challenges in the North are expected to be the panacea in the South. This chapter wants to argue that this is an outcome of chosen epistemic lenses in democratic theory-inspired scholarship in southern Africa, which is also an import of commitment to Eurocentric Western canon in political science.

Even in the context of wide-ranging discussion showing how the transition from liberation movements to parties in many parts of Africa had actually led to one-party regimes or broadly the dominance of society by singular parties. Since the 1970s, African political researchers have analysed the evolution of political regimes in Africa. This points to the failure of democracy to happen or its failure to endure, partly due to the rise of garrison politics with the intervention of military in politics or as a result of failure of parties to deliver on the assumptions of democratic political theory as outlined earlier. Similarly, the African discourses show this disappointment about the state of democracy and its performance in relation to meeting the needs of citizens and in this regard the disappointment extends to political institutions like parties.

There is another strand in the discourses disappointed with the turn of democratic evolution in Africa. It is pretty much part of the dominant political science of democratization (Saul, 1999) manifesting also in the South, i.e. the dominant and Eurocentric discourses with left and right wings as well as radical and conservative strands, which work shift the debates to a centre of gravity loyal to the assumptions of mainstream democratic theory. A key part of this is insisted on narrow confines of the debate around liberal form of multi-partyism and discomfort with traditions emerging from the margins of the western world.

Few have argued the point about liberation movements in power and the need for democratisation on the basis of the idea of modern political parties as much as South African based scholars. Roger Southall, for instance, has written most persuasively about how liberation movements that embodied the hopes and aspirations of the masses as southern Africa transitioned from struggle to democracy, as they put it, became disappointing in power (Southall, 2013). Focusing mainly on the ANC in South Africa, SWAPO in Namibia and ZANU-PF in Zimbabwe, this discourse shows that liberation movements are characterised by paradoxical qualities in being both emancipatory and authoritarian, in the philosophy and political culture of democratic centralism, and in military style nationalist outlook in certain cases. In power, they have used these to capture the state to serve the parochial interests of a clique of liberation movement leadership. They have used noble goals like economic transformation and land reform in order to strengthen their dominance of the multiparty system, thus weakening the democratic nature of the state. They have used their hold on state power to plan themselves as vehicles of total dominance of the public opinion and sentiment.

For this reason, it has been shown that while these once glorious movements have retained their grip on power, using their incumbency sometimes nefariously to remain in power, their ability to drive popular progressive agendas and lead the society through further transformation after colonialism have diminished. The death of liberation movements has already been prophesied (Mashele & Qobo, 2014). This is linked to the dissipation of their moral authority, intellectual prowess, and the woeful failure to run the state efficiently to the chagrin of the ordinary masses for whom the dream of liberation remains elusive.

The liberation movements are perceived to have a character and nature that nurture and entrenches their hegemony as governing parties to the detriment of multiparty democracy. They are accused of employing a range of advantages of incumbency such as control over the distribution of resources, used to reward loyalty and to woe the support of the poor who remain the majority of voters as well as using instruments of crude power in the form of intimidation of critics and political opposition. They are said to have used their struggle credentials to drive race-based politics. Critics argue that they have also actively worked to undermine constitutionalism by weakening aspects of constitutions that are designed to strengthen separation of power, accountability and constrain abuse of executive power. They stand accused for undermining the independence of the judiciary in some countries and parliament in most cases. They are said to have sought to dominate the state by extending their control to civil society, trade unions, business, rural populations and the media. Of course, these tendencies exist to different extent from country to country. The results, however, uniformly point to the consolidation of party-state "in which constitutionality is assailed but fluctuates between competing elites", for the intentions to completely capture the state is also subject to class and ideological contestations within southern African liberation movements (Southall, 2013: 171-3).

"We are reaching an end of an era in southern Africa", argues Southall (2013: 327). Makumbe (2003: 2) concurs that the liberation movements that captured public imagination, achieved widespread popular legitimacy, which they used to ascend to power at independence turned out to be "deeply flawed organisations". While they helped unite the struggle for liberation and unite countries behind a vision of democratic and developmental outcomes after independence, they became fractured and captured by groups of powerful elite with interests other than those declared in their historical documents. They have overtime become obsessed with the total control of the state and society, helping to diminish the democratic credentials of their governance. They have become, as some argue, a major threat to democracy and popular aspirations. Their decline and imminent death are inevitable on this basis. For some this is necessary for the next phase of the evolution of the democratic process to happen.

The liberation struggle, movements and the search for decolonial futures: Conclusions

What this discussion fails to do is to appreciate the fact that what is said to be the case with liberation movements actually applies to political parties on the African continent as well. Political parties have also lost moral compasses, ideological content, policy substance and institutional capacity to build democracies geared at delivering on the popular aspirations. The high-jacking of democracy by a highly selfish political elite, leading to garrison democracy or big man democracy or dominant party democracy has happened both in areas under liberation movements as well as those under modern political parties. Countries that managed to bring down liberation movements such as Malawi and Zambia, for instance, do not have a different experience to those under liberation movements in relation to the points raised in the party dominance debate. Understanding this would have helped the debate to explore beyond the nature and character of liberation movements for answers to: what has happened and what must happen going forward?

Secondly, the discussion does not sufficiently take into account the debates on democracy theory and practice in Africa coming from within Africa, such discussions as have pointed to the important factor of an inherited neo-colonial state and capitalist economy as constraining, distorting, deceiving and complicating factors. The decision to embrace pragmatism led them into adopting neoliberal route to economic futures, which came with disastrous outcomes in relation to poverty, inequality, unemployment and underdevelopment. The choices in this regard, which some acknowledge, were not completely free because the world system pressures underpinned by the "end of history" thesis limited what could be chosen, both for liberation movements and governing parties of other kinds. Samir Amin eloquently illustrates this when he introduces his thesis that there was a liberal virus that re-emerged in the late 20th century whose roots are in the 16th century as follows:

> *The virus caused among its victims a curious schizophrenia. Humans no longer lived as whole beings, organizing themselves to produce what is necessary to satisfy their needs (what the learned have called "economic life") and simultaneously developing the institutions, the rules, and the customs that enable them to develop (what the same learned people have called "political life"), conscious that the two aspects of social life are inseparable. Henceforth, they lived sometimes as homo oeconomicus, abandoning to "the market" the responsibility to regulate their "economic life" automatically, and sometimes as "citizens" depositing in ballot boxes their choices for those who would have the responsibility to establish the rules of the game for their "political life (Amin, 2004: 8).*

While there is a strand of the dominant debate that decry the liberation movements' sinking into the neoliberal disaster (Bond, 2005), but there is an appreciation of the conditions forced upon liberation movements and other governing parties operating in the shadows of the ghosts of empire in relation to choices about state management, economic and social policies, including the use of political conditionality, aid and crude economic measures by the centre of the world system (Mkandawire, 1995; Hutchful, 1995). An insufficient understanding of how coloniality and its matrices of power operate limits our understanding of the schizophrenia Amin alluded to, the paradoxical character of liberation movements Southall identified, the ambiguities of dependence they and other governing parties exhibit.

In this context, there is inadequate consideration of this point that Nzongola-Ntalanja made as far back as 1987, that: "the struggle for genuine liberation involves the transformation of the inherited structures of the state and the economy in order to make them capable of serving the interests of the African workers and peasants"(Nzongola-Ntalanja, 1987: x). Therefore, the failure of the new African bourgeoisie to transform the state and economy in fundamental ways meant that they would use an inherited state system designed for oppression and an unchanged economic system to achieve liberation goals, which was bound to fail. He further links this to the rise of the counter-revolution within Africa and globally, a negative force in which the African political elite became entangled and involved, leading to anti-democratic and anti-people governments. This applies to both political parties and liberation movements, for they are led by the same elite that Frantz Fanon describes as fundamentally driven by a wish to join the imperial bourgeoisie than transformation of societies in the South.

Therefore, the expectation of liberation movements to transition into modern political parties or their replacement with another set of parties would be of no consequence in relation to the evolution towards popular democracy liberation struggles envisaged. The decline of liberation movements for reasons discussed immediately above is obvious and apparent, but the reasons for this are more varied than just the nature of liberation movement conduct. The end of this era does not seem to promise an end to the deferment of dreams and the shuttered expectations in the wake of neo-colonial postcolonial configurations of being, power and knowledge that produces disappointments. Liberation movements suffer the same fate as major political parties in Africa with which they share many similarities including the six challenges that Amilcar Cabral mentions in the Weapon of Theory, namely: a crisis of vision, a death of liberation ideology, a dearth of revolutionary theory, weak policy and programming, internal cleavages/factionalism, a society marked by social and cultural dissonance, and a dominant world that is inimical to national liberation (Zondi, 2018).

In this chapter, our focus was on one widespread view that the failure or reluctance of liberation movements to transition into political parties was a major challenge for democratic consolidation in southern Africa. So, it is not just the character of the leaders that rise within their ranks, as some would argue; neither is it poor policy design and weak focus on implementation of plans, as others would say; but it is their very identity as liberation movements in a post-struggle period that lies at the heart of the problem. This chapter has argued that this view is born out of scepticism about the very idea of liberation movements as an experience and an agency that emerged from the margins of a Western, modern, colonial/neo-colonial and hegemonic world system. We therefore conclude that there is no real value to be derived from transitioning liberation movements into political parties for what is needed is to decolonise the state by fundamentally transforming the inherited political, economic and social systems, and renegotiating the agency of African state in the neoliberal neo-colonial world system.

References

Adejumobi, S. & Olukoshi, A. 2008. Introduction: Transition, continuity and change. In: Adejumobi, S & Olukoshi, A. (eds). The African Union and New Strategies for Development in Africa. New York: Cambria Press. 3–19.

Amin, S. 2004. The Liberal Virus: Permanent War and the Americanization of the World. New York: Monthly Review Press.

Asante, M.K. 2009. Afrocentricity. GES Africa Working Paper. http://www.gesafrica.org/wp-content/uploads/2016/02/Afrocentricity.pdf.

Asante, M.K. 1987. Afrocentricity: The Theory of Social Change. Chicago: Peoples Publishing Group

Bond, P. 2005. US Empire and South African Subimperialism. Socialist Register, no. August 2002. pp. 218-238.

Chege, M. 1992. Remembering Africa. Foreign Affairs, 17 (1): 8–15.

Diamond, L. & Gunther, R. 2001. Political Parties and Democracy. Baltimore: Johns Hopkins University Press.

Dussel, E. 1980. Philosophy of Liberation. New York: Orbis Books.

Edigheji, O. 2005. A Democratic Developmental State in Africa? A Concept Paper, Centre for Policy Studies, Research Report 105. May.

Grosfoguel, R. 2009. A decolonial approach to political-economy: Transmodernity, border thinking and global coloniality. Kult Fall (6): 10–38.

Hountondji, P. 1997. Endogenous Knowledge: Research Trails. Dakar: CODESRIA Books.

Huntington, S.P. 1991. Democracy's Third Wave. Journal of Democracy, 2 (2): 12–34.

Hutchful, E. 1995. The international dimensions of the democratisation process in Africa. In: Chole, E & Ibrahim, J. (eds). Democratisation Processes in Africa: Problems and Prospects. Dakar: CODESRIA Books.

Mafeje, A. 2011. Africanity: A combative ontology. In: Devisch, R. & Nyamnjoh, F.B. (eds). The Postcolonial Turn. Bameda and Leiden: Langaa and African Studies Centre. https://doi.org/10.1353/esc.2015.0089.

Makumbe, J. 2003. Zimbabwe's Turmoil: Problems and Prospects. Pretoria: Institute for Security Studies.

Maloka, E.T. 2001. The South African African renaissance debate: A Critique. Polis RCSP 8: 1–10.

Mashele, P. & M. Qobo. 2014. The Fall of the ANC: What Next? Johannesburg: Picador Africa.

Mills, C.W. 1998. Blackness Visible: Essays on Philosophy and Race. Ithaca and London: Cornell University Press.

Mkandawire, T. 1995. Adjustment, political conditionality and democratisation in Africa. In Democratisation Processes in Africa: Problems and Prospects, edited by Eshetu Chole and Jibrin Ibrahim, 81–99. Dakar: CODESRIA Books.

Mkandawire, T. 2002 Building the African State in the Age of Globalisation. Annual Lecture. Johannesburg. Mapungubwe Institute for strategic Reflection (MISTRA).

Ndlovu-Gatsheni, S.J. 2013. Coloniality of Power in Postcolonial Africa: Myths of Decolonization. Dakar: CODESRIAColon aili.

Norris, P. 2005. Political Parties and Democracy in Theoretical. and Practical Perspectives. Washington: National Democratic Institute for International Affairs.

Nyong'o, P. A. 1987. Popular Struggles for Democracy in Africa. London: Zed Books; United Nations University.

Nzongola-Ntalaja, G. 1997. The state and democracy in Africa. In: Nzongola-Ntalaja, G and Margaret Lee, M. (eds). The State and Democracy in Africa. Harare: AAPS Books.

Nzongola-Ntalanja, G. 1987. Revolution and Counter-Revolution in Africa. London: Zed Books.

Peet, R. 2007. Geography of Power: The Making of Global Economic Policy. New York: Zed Books.

Pennock, J.R. 1979. Democratic Political Theory. New Jersey: Princeton University Press.

Saul, J. 1994. Liberation without Democracy? Rethinking the Experiences of the Southern African Liberation Movements. Wits University.

Saul, J.S. 1999. For fear of being condemned as old fashioned: Liberal democracy versus popular democracy in Sub-Saharan Africa. In: Daddieh, C.K. & Mengisteab, K. (eds). State Building and Democratization in Africa: Faith, Hope and Realities, Westport: Praeger.

Shivji, I. 2003. The Struggle for democracy. https://www.marxists.org/subject/africa/shivji/struggle-democracy.htm

Southall, R. 2013. Liberation Movements in Power: Party and State in Southern Africa. Pietermaritzburg: University of Kwazulu-Natal Press and James Currey.

Stokes, S.C. 1999. Political parties and democracy. Annual Review of Political Science 2: 243–67. https://doi.org/10.1146/annurev.polisci.2.1.243.

Wa Thiong'o, N. 2009. Something Torn and New: An African Renaissance. New York: Basic Books.

Van Biezen, I. & Katz, R.S. 2005. Democracy and political parties. Party Politics, 14 (6): 663-83.

Zeleza, P.T. 2013. Banishing the silences: Towards the globalization of African history. http://erepo.usiu.ac.ke/bitstream/handle/11732/1163/zeleza.

Zondi, S. 2018. The Weapon of Theory: Some Cabralian Theses on the African Political Predicament. Inaugural Lecture. University of Pret

Chapter Three

ANC - led South Africa's health record: An African human rights perspective

Kgothatso Shai and Olusola Ogunnubi

Introduction

The 21st March non-violent campaign against pass laws in South Africa was initially planned to take place on the 31st March 1960 under the guidance of the ANC. This date was chosen for the purpose of giving more meaning and expression to the 31st March anti-pass campaign that took place in the year 1919. However, when information about the ANC's plan to embark on a campaign for the total abolition of the pass laws on the 31st March 1960 leaked and reached PAC members, the leadership of PAC and its constituency decided to stage its own opportunistic campaign ten days before the ANC. This was done in order to take advantage of its tactical, strategic and political significance for the growth of the party that was founded in 1959. Despite the peaceful nature of the 'hijacked' campaign by the PAC, the police in both Sharpeville and Langa meted out violence by firing live ammunition on the protesters. As a result, 69 people were reportedly killed, and 180 others severely wounded in Sharpeville. In the case of Langa, three people were left dead while 26 others suffered serious injuries.

There have been competing explanations by scholars and government officials about the Sharpeville and Langa massacre. An official account by the apartheid regime has been that the campaign in question agitated for violence and instability against the security establishment. It added that the chaotic manner in which police were provoked left them with no option but to crush the protest ruthlessly. On the contrary, the fact that the majority of the victims of Sharpeville and Langa massacres were not armed and were shot on their backs is evidence that they were peaceful. As a results, when charged with a harsh response, they also opted to run for cover, instead of fighting back (Pahad, 2014). While the dynamics of crucial historical events such as the Sharpeville and Langa massacres are contested across the political and academic divide, a quick cursory overview of the academic and popular literature reflects competing positions about post-apartheid South Africa's human rights record in the health sector.

Globally, South Africa features prominently in most health care problems such as HIV/AIDS, Tuberculosis, maternal and child mortality, as well as obesity. These remain the leading cause of death (DEA, 2013).[1] In South Africa, the health burden mostly affects the poor, with the majority of those affected unable to afford private health care services and therefore having to rely on the government for health care support. In over two decades of post-apartheid era, South Africa's mortality and morbidity profile of infectious and non-communicable diseases have worsened considerably among all age groups (Kahn, 2011). Clearly, this calls for a rethinking of the philosophy underpinning the delivery of health care in South Africa and Africa generally. Admittedly, the National Development Plan 2030 makes laudable recommendations on how to effectively improve the socioeconomic determinants of health, address the imbalance that has resulted in unforgivable historical injustices and bridge the embedded inequality in the provision of health care (National Planning Commission, 2012). However, despite annual budgetary expenditure, little has been done to change the status quo in ways that guarantee the human rights of South Africans in such critical arenas as the health sector. It was envisaged that the political progress experienced in South Africa with the enthronement of liberal democracy in 1994 should ultimately translate into significant transformation in all aspects of societal life including the health sector. As Litch and de Villiers (1994: 1) projected, "the evidence of progress we now see ranges from disheartening to uncertain". The present chapter considers the extent to which health care delivery is a guaranteed human right in South Africa.

As a socioeconomic right, health care is secured in the South African Constitution. Evans (2002: 197) explains that health as a human right is captured in the Tavistock Group's principle that, "the right to health cannot be bought and sold in the marketplace like other commodities. Nor can the right to health be limited by the ability to pay". Some scholars proffering a liberal consensus argue against a human right to health (Barlow, 1999). They contest the "definition and extent of both human rights and health care" (Evans, 2002: 197).

The dominant narrative within the academic circles and the mainstream media is that South Africa's health system is in a crisis. The current crisis with the Life Esidimeni tragedy, which resulted in the death of over 94 mental health patients, is a constant reminder of a failing public health system (Kahn, 2011). Furthermore, in Africa, the Ebola virus disease (EVD) outbreak that started in the year 2013 and lasted until 2016 raises serious human rights question about the rife perception of the need to curb diseases originating in the global South from spreading to more prosperous regions and the powerlessness of the former to address this. Durojaiye and Mirugi-Mukundi (2015: 23) warn that Africa's right to health, guaranteed in several human rights instruments, is further compromised by the slowness of pharmaceutical companies in industrialised countries in developing a cure or vaccine for Ebola which "confirms the fact that these companies hardly

---

1 According to the NDP 2030 report, between 1998 and 2008, notification of deaths doubled, reaching a staggering 700,000 per year (NPC 2012).

invest in tropical or neglected diseases that may benefit millions of people in poor regions".

The first part of this chapter details the general orientation of the study. Secondly, the methodological component of the study is advanced. Further sections review the relevant literature on health and human rights focusing on South Africa. It also presents the legal framework in which health care is delivered in the country. The fourth section appraises South Africa's health sector in terms of securing the socioeconomic claims of health as a human right. The final part is the conclusion and policy implications.

Methodological and conceptual issues

It should be emphasized that the epistemic location of this chapter is the Afrocentric paradigm, as propagated by scholars such as Asante (2003), Mazama (2003), Modupe (2003) and Alkebulan (2007). Afrocentricity is relevant for this discourse because most studies on this subject stem from a Euro-American standpoint and do not often correctly capture the qualitative imagery of the human rights discourse of Africa and very often neglect the political history of its people in general. This less considered missing link (Afrocentric perspective) offers deeper analytical rigour for understanding the policy machinery of African countries. This should be understood within the context that policy analysis (and monitoring in particular) requires relevant, reliable and valid information (Shai, 2013: 10). Flowing from this, Don K. Price makes a distinction between scientific estate, which seeks only to discover knowledge, and the professional estate, which strives to apply scientific knowledge to the solution of practical problems. Based on the foregoing, it is proposed that the African situation should be perceived, interpreted and understood in the first instance through an indigenous theoretical lens, tools and standards, if Africa is to find lasting solutions to challenges faced by its people and countries. This proposition finds a true and perhaps honest expression in the works of many African-centred scholars. For example, Richards (1979: 249) lends credence to the theoretical attitude and exposition of this chapter when she asserts that:

> It would be the mission of African social scientists, at home and in the Diaspora, to devote their energies to the radical reconstruction of the disciplines in which they were trained. Without such an approach, African peoples run the risk of incorporating the theoretical, mythological and ideological models of white social science into their own methodologies, thereby unknowingly internalising the values of western European society, including the negative image of Africa which white racialism and culturalism has created.

In terms of the research design, this chapter is largely based on document analysis. Equally important, the current chapter emphatically projects human rights as the inherent and inalienable rights of the people in order for them to be treated with equality, dignity, and respect. Human rights are normally entrenched in law – whether international or national law – with the United Nations (UN) as the custodian for their promotion, protection, and realization.[2] States, on the other hand, have a responsibility to ensure the enjoyment of human rights by all citizens. In essence, they are expected to make provision for the respect, promotion, and adherence of human rights into their domestic laws and policies. It should be taken into consideration that it is not every country in the world where these rights are respected and preserved (Shai & Mothibi, 2015). As such, the analysis of this chapter deliberately uses South Africa as a test case to provide a nuanced Afrocentric appraisal of Africa's health system, as well as its connection with human rights in the post-Millennium Development Goals (MDGs) era. Although the focus of this chapter is on South Africa, it is argued that the country's human rights record in the health sector can be well understood if it is located within a broader African context.

Legislative frameworks on health care: Between theory and practice

There are widespread claims in the literature that there has been tremendous progress in the protection of human rights since the establishment of the UN and the Commission on Human Rights over 65 years ago (Evans, 2002). However, this discourse is often challenged by the reality of the deplorable health conditions in many African countries. Within government circles, it is believed that major strides have been made to provide better health services for all. Nevertheless, despite numerous policy provisions and budgetary spending on health care, as well as the guarantees of the Constitution enshrining basic health care as a fundamental human right, inadequate health care remains a lingering problem for many South Africans. Based on the preceding polarised views about these public health and human rights, this chapter seeks to expand the disciplinary engagement of South Africa's human rights record in the health sector using an Afrocentric perspective.

Chapter 2 of the South African 1996 Constitution, the Bill of Rights entrenches human rights in the country's national law. In terms of the provision of health, as part of these rights, Act 108, section 27 provides that: Everyone has the right to have access to – (a) health care services, including reproductive health care; The state must take reasonable legislative and other measures within its available resources, to achieve the progressive realisation of each of these rights. Read with section 9: (3), the supreme law of the country further asserts that "The state may not unfairly discriminate directly or indirectly against anyone on one or more grounds, including race, gender, sex, pregnancy, marital status, ethnic or social origin, colour, sexual orientation, age, disability, religion, conscience, belief, culture, language, and birth; No person may unfairly discriminate directly or indirectly against anyone on one or more grounds in terms of sub-section (3). A number of policies further corroborate the constitutional provision guaranteeing the equality of health care access to South Africans. For instance, Chapter 10 of

---

2. Article 12 of the International Covenant on Economic, Social and Cultural Rights (ICESCR) makes broad provisions guaranteeing the right to highest attainable standard of physical and mental health of every individual.

the National Development Plan 2030 on "Promoting Health" articulates reform strategies aimed to achieve nine long-term health goals for South Africa, which includes the following:

- Increase average male and female life expectancy to 70 years

- Progressively improve TB prevention and cure

- Reduce maternal, infant and child mortality

- Significantly reduce prevalence of non-communicable chronic diseases

- Reduce injury, accidents and violence by 50 percent from 2010 levels

- Complete health systems reforms

- Primary healthcare teams provide care to families and communities

- Universal health care coverage

- Fill posts with skilled, committed and competent individuals (National Planning Commission, 2012)

However, the distinct overlap between equality and health rights immediately exposes ethical dilemma for an economically, culturally and sexually diverse society such as South Africa. As the NDP 2030 outlines, "The performance of South Africa's health system since 1994 has been poor, despite good policy and relatively high spending as a proportion of GDP"(National Planning Commission, 2012: 331). It is for this reason that part of the nine challenges that necessitated the development of the NDP 2030 included the failure of the public health system to meet the demand of the country and sustain quality. Related to this has been dwindling funding of the health sector, which shows a lack of prioritization of health as a critical aspect of national well-being. For example, budgetary allocation to health care relative to GDP over a period of seven years shows a declining trend of a chronically underfunded sector (see Table 1).

Table 1: South Africa's Government Health Expenditure 2007 – 2014

Year	Total (Rand million)	% of GDP	% of total government expenditure
2007/08	71,439	3.4	13.9
2008/09	85,154	3.7	14.0
2009/10	99,468	4.1	13.8
2010/11	109,769	4.1	14.1
2011/12	122,427	4.2	14.7
2012/13	132,165	4.0	14.7
2013/14	140,721	4.0	14.6

Source: Authors' compilation; see (National Planning Commission, 2012).

There is no gainsaying that like everyone else Lesbian, Gay, Bisexual,

Transgender and Intersex (LGBTI) groups are also entitled to benefit from these rights and others, as enshrined in the Constitution and related laws of South Africa. However, the realities and practicalities in South Africa show a widening chasm between theoretical prescriptions of health delivery and practice in this regard. Indeed, despite extant laws guaranteeing the rights of the LGBTI community, it is common knowledge among most South Africans that the LGTBI populace in South Africa is often subjected to unfair discrimination, persecution, and violence for merely expressing who they are and who they choose to love. The foregoing should be understood within the context of the Rational Comprehensive model of policy analysis; which explains that there are usually no societal values agreed upon. On the contrary, there are only benefits to specific groups and individuals, many of which are conflicting (Dunn, 2015). Since conflicting benefits and costs cannot be compared or weighed, it is significant for the society, in general, to make certain ethical sacrifices and compromises for the sake of mutual and peaceful co-existence, stability, security, and development (Maake, 2009).

While the literature on health and human right is rife and its study in South Africa is not new, not much research has been undertaken in this respect. For instance, scholars have researched on the dimension of South Africa's response to HIV as a human right issue. This raises the need for social and economic rights of the people to be promoted on the same level as the civil and political rights guaranteed in the Bill of Rights (Heywood & Cornell, 1998).

South Africa's health sector: Comparative national, continental and global prognosis

The contemporary society and the Africa-West praxis manifest a double-edged sword. However, unlike the post-independent African state, the West and the United States of America (US) tend to interfere unnessarily in the affairs of other countries, as were the cases in Iraq (2003) and Libya (2011) (Poopedi, 2014; Shai, 2010). However, when it comes to their nationals, the US and other Western countries are generally delicate, kind and careful. In contrast, most African leaders are directly (and in complicit) cruel to their people. For example, Swaziland (current), Zimbabwe (2008) (Dzimiri, Runhare, Dzimiri, & Mazorodze, 2014; Maleka & Shai, 2016). This is an important point that distinguishes African leaders from Western leaders. The above discussion is corroborated by Onyeani (2012: 38) in his claim that "in Africa, we are totally undisciplined. We have leaders who are not ruthless with themselves in pursuit of excellence but who are quick being ruthless to their citizens".

Contextually, nationalist leaders have tried to win the hearts and minds of the masses to support the cauldron of the struggle against the inhumane and brutal systems of colonialism, imperialism and apartheid. In order to do so, these leaders made promises ranging from better education, gainful employment and decent medical health care in post-independence era and new democratic dispensation (as in the case of South Africa) (Khapoya, 2010). It is for this reason that education, labour and health rights have been effected in the policy framework of the post-independent African state (Shai & Molapo, 2017). Despite this, severe contradictions are evident regarding the seriousness of African states and governments in rolling out health services. Admittedly, health is an essential socioeconomic service in South Africa. However, in Africa as a whole, the health sector is riddled with structural problems relating to innovation, accessibility, and trade. In the African situation, respective national and provincial governments usually only show real commitment to the provision of health services when the effects of disasters such as HIV/AIDS and Ebola reach alarming proportions. Even then, Westerners typically lead mitigating efforts for addressing worsening health situations in South Africa and elsewhere in Africa. To make matters worse, even essential amenities used in South Africa/Africa's health facilities (such as antibiotics, injections and intravenous infusions) are often imported and without any remarkable effort to produce the same within the continent (Onyeani, 2012).

Lack of political will

The deplorable situation of Africa's health security is compounded by an already worse situation, exemplified for instance in limited progress relating to the establishment of the only medical school to be established in the new democratic dispensation. Following the detachment of the Medunsa campus from the University of Limpopo, the new medical school was scheduled to be attached to the latter. According to government reports, the University of Limpopo's medical school was opened for its first intake during the 2016 academic year (Quintal, 2016). However, as recent media reports about the medical school indicate, it is safe to state that there are serious structural weaknesses that make it impossible for the University to produce globally competitive medical doctors, at least in the short run. This distasteful situation is a disservice to aspiring medical doctors registered at the institution. It is also a dream deferred for the communities in Limpopo province, who had pinned their hopes on the University of Limpopo's medical school to produce locally relevant and globally competitive medical doctors, to ameliorate the critical shortages of senior medical staff at public hospitals. It would appear that the failure of the government to ensure that the medical school at the University of Limpopo (a 2nd historically disadvantaged university earmarked for the training of medical doctors) is established to the level of full functionality can be partly attributed to the fact that the manner in which it was launched was driven by less political will and developmental commitment. Furthermore, its establishment was prompted by a desperate desire to score cheap political points for the governing ANC and quench the selfish interests of certain individuals who stood to financially benefit from this project by doing business with the university either legally or illegally. It is also not a far-fetched idea that the performance bonuses of the university's senior administrators and the public relations rewards cannot be wholly de-linked from the speed at which the medical school at the University of Limpopo was pre-maturely operationalised.

Burdening health insurance

Meanwhile, it is also interesting to note that in South Africa, a health insurance policy is expensive while a funeral cover policy is comparatively cheap. For instance, the lowest monthly premium for health cover is around R600 per person (depending on the benefits) (Bonitas, 2015). On the other hand, it is possible to secure a funeral cover policy for as little as R120.00 per person (but also depending on age and benefits) (Clientele Life Insurance, 2015). What can be deduced from this contradiction is that while South Africa's government and the private sector seem to be concerned about giving decent funerals to the people, there is a small premium for preserving their health conditions. By logical corollary, this unfortunate trend should be worrying to all; considering the fact that health is a crucial pillar of socio-economic development. The irony is that while South Africa is internationally lauded for having one of the best Constitution and laws, especially in terms of guaranteeing people's rights, with a ranking of 131st, its workforce is undoubtedly one of the unhealthiest globally (World Health Organisation, 2015).

It is interesting to note that South Africa's developmental state is modelled along China, where it takes only ten minutes to see a medical doctor in a private health facility (xi, 2014). This is a situation that is highly commendable about the communist society of China and which is hardly observable in African countries, including South Africa. In contrast, the depth of the disappointing state of South Africa's health system is also reinforced by the fact that in South Africa, as it is with many African states, pizza delivery is often faster than an emergency callout for an ambulance. A narrow view of the sorry state of South Africa's health sector attributes this to rampant corruption. However, a sober reflection of the state of governance in South Africa *vis-à-vis* China shows that corruption knows no boundaries. In fact, corruption in China is rife or worse than in African countries. To add to this heated scholarly and policy discourse, Nkondo (2012) observes that:

> Corruption knows no bounds. It does not disappear as economies grow. Instead, it assumes new forms. For corruption is symptomatic of a deeper systemic problem, the failure of the public-private-partnerships that African governments have sought to mediate the contradictory claims of democracy and the market, a failure that has created a virtual collusive system between political and business elites.

Confused declarations

Central to the problems faced by post-independent African states is the tendency to make 'declarations without real action'. Moreover, the deplorable working conditions in most African states naturally pushes medical doctors and other health professionals to go and serve in countries such as Australia, US and Britain. Unfortunately, this trend results in brain drain for South Africa and other African countries. But it can also be understood as 'brain gain' for the receiving industrialised countries. It is therefore not surprising that globally, Africa has the second-worst shortage of health workers at 4.2 million, compared to Europe's 100,000 (World Health Organisation, 2017).

Despite the complex web of political and socio-economic challenges faced by South Africa in particular and Africa in general, the exiled President of the ANC, Oliver Tambo (as cited by (Pahad, 2014: 80) advises that "[T]o be true to history, we must concede that there have been difficulties as well as triumphs along our part …". Flowing from this, it is indeed necessary to appreciate the achievements regarding South Africa's political transition. However, it must also be honestly acknowledged that there are persistent challenges in health, economy, and society in general. Sadly, in the recent past, several leaders of African states have died either in domestic private hospitals or outside their countries in their search for better health service. Apart from Robert Gabriel Mugabe, the late former president of Zimbabwe who died in Singapore in 2019, other examples include Michael Sata of Zambia who died in Britain; Umara Yar'Adua who passed away in 2010 after months of hospitalisation in Saudi Arabia; Meles Zenawi of Ethiopia who died in Belgium. In relation to this, Motshegoa (2014) has noted that the recent death of Michael Sata has brought 'the number of African presidents dying in foreign hospitals to nine'. As Kazeem (2017) notes, "Indeed, in the last decade, six of the 12 African leaders who have died while in office did so while seeking treatment abroad". It is the conviction of this chapter that the passing away of most African leaders outside their countries and/or in private hospitals is a tragic acknowledgment of their inability and/or unwillingness to adequately address the health needs and demands of their down-trodden and impoverished civilian populace.

Table 2: African presidents that died in foreign private hospitals

President	Country	Died
Michael Sata	Zambia	London (2014)
Malam Bacai Sanhá	Guinea Bissau	France (2012)
Meles Zenawi	Ethiopia	Belgium (2012)
Omar Bongo	Gabon	Spain (2009)
Levy Mwanawasa	Zambia	France (2008)
Bingu wa Mutharika	Malawi	South Africa (2013)

Source: Kazeem (2017)

The preceding narrative of the sad reality of the status quo of African health sector affirms this chapter's argument that inadequate health services in the public sector deny the majority of people the opportunity to enjoy their health rights and human rights broadly. Historicising the negative state of health in South Africa and elsewhere in the continent reflects a mixed bag of both internal and external factors. These factors have contributed to the appalling situation (Chazan, 1988). At the root of this problem is neo-colonialist tendencies, championed by the West, to the disadvantage of African nations. For example, in the post-independence era, most African states signed some agreements with the West, which continue to deprive the African masses of what is due to them. An example are the agreements that have produced the unpopular Structural Adjustment Programmes (SAPs) and Poverty Reduction Papers (PRPs) of both the International Monetary Fund (IMF) and World Bank, which have further deepened Africa's developmental crisis as opposed to their envisaged goals (Shai, 2013).

These agreements have provided a safe passage for African states to access foreign aid (either in the form of loans or grants), but with stifling conditions. This aid was meant to help Africa address its political, economic and social problems. However, conditional aid has generally failed to emancipate Africa from the shackles of poverty and under-development. Hence, foreign aid has been abused by the West to eschew the policy content and direction of many of the African states towards a particular agenda. Often this agenda does not serve the interests of the local people. In post-apartheid South Africa, for example, the Mandela Administration was compelled by the Western capitalist donors to ditch the socialist orientated Reconstruction and Development Programme (RDP), as the macroeconomic policy framework of the country (Shai, 2009). As a result, in 1996 the ANC-led government switched the RDP in favour of the more liberal flavoured Growth, Employment, and Redistribution (GEAR) strategy to please the West and ultimately gain foreign investor confidence.

As in other African countries, South Africa's decision to conform to demands of the globalising economy has literally undermined the legitimate aspirations of the locals to receive adequate health care. Hence, South Africa's government was discouraged by the donor community from making huge investments to provide free social services such as adequate health care and decent education. Consequently, there is an evolving contradictory trend which has produced a crisis in public health services for the majority and decent private health services for the few, privileged minorities[3] suggest that human rights have been *commodified* in the new South Africa. Undoubtedly, skewed imbalances in spending in both private and public sectors have led to increased costs and adversely affected the distribution of services. This has further conscripted the delivery and guarantee of socioeconomic human rights of the people, as provided for in the Constitution (National Planning Commission, 2012).

This chapter further argues that progress in the recognition of international human rights must transcend beyond the ratification of international treaties and regimes. In addition, more attention needs to be focused on the massive population of the African people that remain secluded from decent health care delivery as a result of prevailing neo-liberal imperatives that dictate national priorities. This therefore calls for a need to secure the acceptance of health and reproductive rights as critical components of human rights. Clearly, as Evans (2002) also believes, the dominant discourse in the international literature is still staged by a liberal consensus on human rights. Thus, the securitization of health in Africa can only be guaranteed when the physical health conditions of its people improve in ways that equally progress their socioeconomic conditions. This Afrocentric narrative perhaps presents a critical alternative argument on the

---

3. The NDP 2030 reports that the country's public sector serves 83 percent (41.7 million) of the population compared to the private sector's 17 percent (8.3 million) (NPC, 2012).

discourse of health as a human right, which is often silenced in popular literature on public health and human rights. Surely, the right to health cannot remain an aspirational claim to human rights, as the liberal consensus school wants us to believe. However, the health consequences of globalisation brought about by the liberal, free market economy continues to dictate "health markets, technologies, science, drugs and the global organisation of business and finance", to the detriment of Africa (Evans, 2002: 213). Pointedly, the intervening features of today's globalised world persist in forms that limit Africa's capacity to secure the socioeconomic rights of its people especially in the area of health care. As Evans (2002: 213) concedes, "Like all other socioeconomic rights, the right to health cannot be realised unless the institutions of the current global order have the capacity to intervene in the activities of those who currently exercise their freedoms to increase their wealth, no matter the social conditions that others must suffer".

To this end, (reproductive) health rights of women must be safeguarded through policy initiatives and adequate budgetary allocation. It is in this context that the World Population Report (2017) calls for the development of legislation on affirmative action, to ensure the prioritization of women's human rights, especially in Africa. Affordability and equality in health care support will continue to remain a huge problem for South Africa and indeed the rest of Africa, until critical reforms are introduced which prioritize Africa and holistically cater for the massive black population that remains in the periphery of health care delivery. Critical to this is the need to comprehensively address the socio-economic determinants that affect health care delivery in South Africa.

Conclusion and policy implications

In the final analysis, it is needless to mention that in the new democratic dispensation, South Africa has been able to steer the political transition successfully. This is due to the reasons outlined in this chapter; namely, that the South African government has not been able to revolutionize its society, including the health sector. As such, human rights are not equally enjoyed by all, as envisaged in the Constitution. While institutionalized racism has been officially abolished in the early 1990s, its manifest challenges continue to persist to date, and remain evident in gaining access to health care. This limitation must be understood within the context that the majoritarian poor and downtrodden civilian populace are still subjected to poor conditions of health services in the public sector while the minority segment of the middle class and wealthy people (who are mostly white) have unparalleled access to decent health services in private facilities. To this end and no matter what the dictates of the international economic and political system project, it is quite important for South Africa to engage robustly on the mobilisation of both economic and human resources, to effectively address its health crisis and enforce equity in the provision of health services. This is a measure that will go a long way in ensuring that the South African state lives up to the people's rights, as enshrined in its Constitution. Lastly, the critical study of this chapter has revealed that South Africa's health system still faces challenges relating to financing inequalities, health literacy and *inter alia*. Equally, there have been improvements in terms of health infrastructure and access to primary health care. Therefore, based on the combination of the above, it is safe to state that South Africa's human rights record in the health sector is at crossroads, but more still needs to be done.

Based on the findings of this study, the following policy recommendations are proposed for consideration by decision makers:

- There is an urgent need for the establishment and tangible support for domestic pharmaceutical companies which will prioritise the needs and interests of the local masses, as compared to their commercially-driven and exploitative Western counterparts.

- While it is useful for South Africa to benchmark globally, it is also important to contextualise such in the African continent, with countries that have common political and socio-economic history with the former.

- Practical measures to contain the scourge of systemic corruption must be considered. This is because corruption eats away from budgets meant to benefit the masses for the benefit of the politically connected few.

- Government must re-prioritize health as a critical aspect of national well-being in terms of quality, budgeting, skills development, recruitment and retention.

- Tangibly criminalise the collusion between the political and business elites in view of gradually untangling democracy from the market.

- Decision makers must be flexible enough to embrace African-centred, emerging and alternative ways of viewing, thinking and acting.

- As a socio-economic right, health must be elevated to the status of civil and political rights that warrant international intervention whenever they are seriously abused.

- Finally, it is strategically and ideologically crucial for [South] African decision makers to transcend political populism in order to stay relevant to the transformation agenda of their society.

References

Alkebulan, A. A. 2007. Defending the paradigm. Journal of Black Studies, 37(3): 410-427.

Asante, M. 2003. Afrocentricity: The Theory of Social Change: African American Images: Chicago, Illinois, US.

Barlow, P. 1999. Health care is not a human right. British Medical Journal, 319 (7205); 321.

Bonitas. 2015. Product offering.

Chazan, N. et al., 1988. Politics and Society in Contemporary Africa. Houndmills, Basingstoke, Hampshire: Macmillan.

Clientele Life Insurance. 2015. Affordable Funeral Cover [Press release]. Retrieved from http://www.clientelelifeinsurance.co.za/?sourceID=3&campaignID=10

DEA. 2013. Annual Report. Pretoria: DEA.

Dunn, W.N. 2015. Public Policy Analysis. New York: Prentice Hall.

Durojaiye, E.T. & Mirugi-Mukundi, G. 2015. The ebola virus and human rights concerns in Africa. African Journal of Reproductive Health, 19(3):18-26.

Dzimiri, P., Runhare, T., Dzimiri, C. & Mazorodze, W. 2014. Naming, identity, politics and violence in Zimbabwe. Studies of Tribes and Tribals, 12(2); 227-238.

Evans, T. 2002. A human right to health? Third World Quarterly, 23(2): 197-215.

Heywood, M. & Cornell, M. 1998. Human rights and AIDS in South Africa: From right margin to left margin. Health and Human Rights, 60-82.

Kahn, K. 2011. Population health in South Africa: Dynamics over the past two decades. Journal of Public Health Policy, 32(1): S30-S36.

Kazeem, Y. 2017. Africa's presidents keep going abroad for medical treatment rather than fixing healthcare at home. Quartz Africa. June 30.

Litch, R. & de Villiers, B. 1994. Introduction. In: South Africa's Crisis of Constitutional Democracy. Litch, R. & de Villiers, B. Washington: AEI Press.

Maake, M. 2009. The Darfur conflict: Reflections on the state of human security since 2003. Unpublished BA Hons (IR) mini-dissertation. Thohoyandou: University of Venda.

Maleka, M.S. & Shai, K.B. 2016. South Africa's post-apartheid foreign policy towards Swaziland. Journal of Public Administration, *51*(2); 194-204.

Mazama, A. 2003. The Afrocentric Paradigm. Trenton: Africa World Press.

Modupe, D.S. 2003. The Afrocentric philosophical perspective: A narrative outline. In: Mazama, A. The Afrocentric Paradigm. Trenton: Africa World Press.

Motshegoa, T. 2014. The Sad reality of African affairs. *Sowetan,* 10 November

National Planning Commission, NPC. 2012. National Development Plan 2030: Our future make it work. Pretoria: National Planning Commission.

Nkondo, M. 2012. Setting the platform for 2014 elections - Born frees learning from veterans: Talking about the future of fundamental change in South Africa. Paper presented at the Seminar organised by the Independent Electoral Commission (IEC), Polokwane.

Onyeani, C. 2012. Capitalist Nigger: The Road to Success: A Spider Web Doctrine. New York: Timbuktu Publishers.

Pahad, A. 2014. Insurgent Diplomat-Civil Talks or Civil War? Johanneburg: Random House Struik.

Poopedi, T.M. 2014. Re-evaluating the African Union's role in resolving conflicts: A case study of Libya. Unpublished BA Hons mini-dissertation. Sovenga: University of Limpopo.

Quintal, G. 2016. New medical school opens in Limpopo. *News24*. Retrieved from *https://www.news24.com/SouthAfrica/News/new-medical-school-opens-in-limpopo-20160216*

Richards, D. 1979. The ideology of European dominance. Présence Africaine, (3): 3-18.

Shai, K.B. 2009. Rethinking United States-South Africa Relations. Hoedspruit: Royal Batubatse Foundation.

Shai, K.B 2010. The United States of America's foreign policy towards Africa: The case studies of Kenya and Nigeria, 1990-2008. Unpublished MA dissertation. Thohoyandou: University of Venda.

Shai, K.B. 2013. A Reader: Public Policy Analysis. Sovenga: University of Limpopo.

Shai, K.B. & Mothibi, K.A. 2015. Describing pre-2009 xenophobic violence in South Africa: A human right perspective. Paper presented at the African Governance: Society, Human Migration, State, Xenophobia and Business Contestations, The Ranch Resort, South Africa.

Shai, K.B. & Molapo, R.R. 2017. The "decriminalisation" of the #FeesMustFall movement in South Africa: An Asantean Perspective. Commonwealth Youth and Development, 15(1): 1-16

World Health Organisation, WHO. 2015. *A Universal Truth: No Health Without a Workforce*. Retrieved from *http://www.who.int/workforcealliance/knowledge/resources/GHWA-a_universal_truth_report.pdf*

World Health Organisation, WHO. 2017. Estimates of health workers needs-based shortages by WHO region, 2013. Retrieved from *http://www.who.int/gho/health_workforce/hrh_012.jpg?ua=1*

Xi, J. 2014. *The Governance of China.* Beijing: Foreign Languages Press.

Chapter Four

Appraising JG Zuma-led ANC through an Afrocentric lens

Kgothatso Shai and Emeka Ndaguba

Introduction

The year 2017 was a defining moment in the context of the liberation history of Africa in general; and the political history of the ANC of South Africa, in particular. It is in this year that Africa's oldest liberation movement and South Africa's ruling political party celebrated 105 years anniversary since its establishment during the year 1912, in Mangaung, Bloemfontein. The year 2017 also marked 23 years since the ANC came to power in the year 1994. Related to this, it is in the year 2017 that the ANC also hosted yet another watershed 54th elective national conference post-Nelson Mandela's death in 2013. Since Jacob Zuma did not avail himself for 3rd term of office as the President of the ANC; the much-anticipated December 2017 national conference ultimately produced his successor as the party leader and subsequently, the 1st citizen of South Africa. Hence, it is in the tradition of the ANC that its President should also serve as its candidate for the Presidency of the country. The premise that Zuma's successor in the ANC would become the country's substantive President is conditional upon a number of factors. Among them, the ability of the ANC to regenerate itself before the year 2019 general elections so that it can retain its dominance of South Africa's political landscape following shreds of electoral misfortunes during the 2016 local government polls. For the purpose of this chapter, the incumbent Cyril Ramaphosa is understood as a caretaker state president for the remainder of the ANC's term of office that officially ends in the year 2019.

There are some in the ANC and beyond who believe that this party's recent electoral misfortunes in areas such as the City of Tshwane, Johannesburg and Nelson Mandela Bay Metropolitan municipalities is largely tied to the roughed moral fibre of its leadership (Mokgosi & Shai, 2016). The Nkandla debacle, corporate capture of state, the shenanigans in state owned enterprises such as South African Airways (SAA), South African Broadcasting Corporation (SABC), Eskom and rampant political corruption is emblematic of the extent of the breakdown in the morality of Jacob-Zuma led ANC (Isike & Ogunnubi, 2017). The cauldron of ills within the circles of the government presided by ANC's

Zuma has served as a fertile ground for widespread calls for him and to particular extent, the erstwhile National Executive Committee (NEC) of the party to step down. The whipping of the NEC in certain circles should be understood within the context that for quite some time it has consistently demonstrated unwillingness or inability to act against Zuma and his allies' misdemeanours. The perceived lack of political goodwill on the part of the ANC NEC to openly renounce obvious wrongdoings on the part of Zuma, friends and his political cronies was generally viewed as symptomatic of the arrogance of the national leadership of the party. However, the factional manner in which the Integrity Committee of the NEC was constituted has rendered it inconceivable for such a structure to effectively summon and discipline then sitting president of the ANC like Zuma.

Zuma's scandals were believed by some in the ANC and outside as the epitome of some of the potential voters' decision to stay away from the polls or cast their votes in favour of the alternative political opposition (Mokgosi & Shai, 2016). Whether this argument is true or simply biased, it was openly dismissed by some prominent ANC leaders who were for "collective responsibility" approach in regard of the decline in electoral support of the ANC. The foregoing analysis suggests that the challenges and problems facing the ANC are many and complex; and surely cannot be wholly attributed to an individual. But this narrative fails to underscore the reality of the centrality of perceptions in voting patterns in South Africa and Africa at large (Fakir & Holland, 2011). This chapter's take on the latter narrative is that its pioneers are fully conscious of the influence of perceptions in voting. But they opted to be economic with the truth in order to protect their personal and factional interests. While Zuma was politically strong, smart and well-calculative in his own right; the fact that most NEC members were members of his cabinet implied that their fate was also tied to his presidency. This situation was a boon for his short-term political survival. We argue that it also constituted a threat to the dominance of the ANC in the long run.

Emerging from the above, it is clear that the discourse on the politics of Zuma led ANC is characterised by deep seated competing perspectives; which are largely rooted within the Western paradigm. As such, this Afrocentric chapter seeks to contribute to this discourse by exploring whether ANC under Zuma represented a stage of degeneration or regeneration for the party. If Zuma's presidency represented degeneration of his party; what are the prospects of the ANC for self-correction and renewal? Revisiting this subject with an alternative theoretical lens (Afrocentricity) from outside the party is important (Asante, 1990). This is especially the case that despite the backdrop of recent electoral misfortunes, the dominant narrative from within the party is that the ANC is like an ocean and it is capable of cleansing and regenerating itself. This may be historically and philosophically correct; but honest lessons from the 2016 local government elections have taught us that opposition forces are capable of successfully coalescing and dislodging the ANC from the mantle of power. The following section of the chapter discusses the blend of research methodology and theory that foregrounds it.

Methodological and theoretical framing

The epistemic location of this chapter is the Afrocentric paradigm. The Afrocentric paradigm is understood and introduced in this chapter as a re-enforcer of the qualitative research paradigm (Shai, 2017). This paradigm was found by this author to be appropriate for this chapter because it permits the cross-following of both empirical and non-empirical methods in research, while remaining culturally sensitive and contextually relevant (Burke, 1991). In other words, and for the purpose of this chapter, the binary logic of knowledge production (i.e. as empirical or non-empirical; subjective or objective; good or evil) is dismissed theoretically and philosophically (Asante, 2003; Chilisa, 2012; Maserumule, 2011). Taking a leaf from Burke (1990) and Buthelezi (2015), we have analysed written text on the political history of the ANC and our personal experience on the practice of South African politics after the year 1994 to primarily answer the central research question of this chapter: Did the ANC under Jacob Zuma represents a stage of degeneration or regeneration for the party? In this regard, the following three steps in discourse analysis as elucidated by Norman Fairclough (as cited by Horvath, 2014) were applied: Description, interpretation and explanation. Firstly, description focused on the formal properties of the text. Secondly, interpretation centred on the nexus between text and interaction with the author. This entails the viewing of a text as an outcome of the production process and as a resource in interpretation. Thirdly and lastly, explanation examined the link between interaction and social context - with the social determination of the production and interpretation processes, and their social effects.

The emerging discourse from the steps outlined above was complemented by the synthesis of available preliminary findings on the central research question of this chapter with the principles of Afrocentricity (Modupe, 2003). In this chapter, the principles of Afrocentricity are embraced and used as the analytical categories for painting a comprehensive picture of the state and health of the ANC under Zuma. The debate about discourse analysis is very extensive and making just literature review in this subject is inconceivable, except drawing few influential citations. According to Lynch (2007: 499) 'discourse analysis' is an umbrella term for several social scientific methods linked with critical theory (African critical theory), cultural and political studies and related disciplines. In a quest to legitimate the common and shared objective of discourse studies, Van Dijk (2001: 352) explains discourse analysis as an "analytical research that primarily studies the way social power abuse, dominance, and inequality are enacted, reproduced, and resisted by text and talk in social and political context". To a certain extent, Van Dijk's (2001) account of discourse studies suggests that conversation analysis can be understood as an extension of discourse analysis. Given the thick description proffered discourse analysis, there is no gainsaying that the latter "is an alternative method, designed for descriptive adequacy, if not objectivity" (Lynch, 2007: 502). While analysis has been done in some of the texts (secondary) reviewed, Lynch (2007: 512) takes the argument further by acknowledging that irrespective of whether such an analysis (un)fits the aims of the professional analyst, "the latter analyst cannot be indifferent to it". Contextually, Van Dijk (2001: 353) outlines the following as some of the fundamental features of discourse analysis:

- It must be better than other studies in order to gain recognition,

- It must be centred on social and political issues, rather than current paradigms,

- Explains discourse structures in terms of properties of social interaction, and

- The primary focus is on the ways discourse structures enact, confirm, reproduce, or challenge relations of power and dominance in society.

Besides surveying the existing literature in this field to avoid the replication of existing arguments and to also, sharpen the theoretical framework of this chapter as mentioned above, the place and role of literature review in this section of the paper is that of a data collection technique. Also denominated as document study (including newspapers), literature review is understood by Mabelebele (2008: 40) as having a huge potential to enrich the amount of data to be analysed. In the same line of reasoning, Leedy & Ormrod (2013: 51) enunciated that:

> Those who have conducted research before you belong to a community of scholars, each of whom has journeyed into the unknown to bring back an insight, a truth, [and] a point of light. What they have recorded of their journeys and findings will make it easier for you to explore the unknown: to help you also discover an insight, a truth, or a point of light.

Meanwhile, the following section of the chapter is an exposition of some of the critical economic factors that have shaped the current trajectory of the ANC. Drawing on the liberalists' propagation that economics is the basis of politics; it is sensible at this juncture to reflect on how economic dynamics in South Africa and the world at large has influenced the growth or degeneration of the ANC under Zuma (Jackson & Sorensen, 2003).

Economic influence on the state of the ANC

The current composition of South African voters' roll entails a fair share of citizens who were born after the dawn of democracy in the year 1994 (Shai, 2015). This is political and demographic development that cannot be overlooked by ANC's election strategists. Hence, the so-called "born frees" do not have emotional links and attachment to the ANC (Nkondo, 2012). They need descent jobs, adequate medical care; and free, decolonised and quality higher education (Khapoya, 2010; Lushaba, 2016; Mekoa, 2016). The failure of the ANC-led government to provide such basic necessities naturally alienates the party and government from the born frees, who have never experienced the full might of apartheid. The exaggerated and biased narrative about the contribution of the ANC in the liberation of South Africa makes less sense to them.

Moreover, money has eroded the pre-1994 political culture of the ANC which was based on the philosophy of humanity (Ubuntu/botho in Nguni/Sotho languages). Among others, this culture was foregrounded on the principles of self-sacrifice, selfless commitment to the people, cooperation and interdependence (Shai, 2016). Currently, there is a notion in the ANC leadership circles that "it is now the turn/time to eat". It is such un-ANC tendencies that have entrenched corruption, fraud, embezzlement of public funds, nepotism and money laundering within the government circles. Hence, such ill-practices were also common in the apartheid government but they were perpetuated in a sophisticated manner that spared the ruling party at the time from declining support; especially from its traditional support base (white population). Any form of culture is not static, be it political or anthropological. As such, the pressures of the neo-liberal global order and the changing political climate of South Africa has prevailed a remarkable metamorphosis of the political culture that defined the ANC as a liberation movement (Shai & Iroanya, 2014).

Hence, during the apartheid era serving in the leadership or ordinarily belonging to the membership of the ANC carried a lot of personal risks than financial gains. It is on this basis that individualism and competition for leadership positions was not germane to the political culture of the ANC. The absence of obvious financial benefits in serving in the leadership of the ANC was central to the maintenance of the party's unity and cohesion. However, the economic security that came with serving in the leadership of the ANC post-1994 has created a fertile ground for factionalism; a phenomenon which has planted seeds of patronage, clientelism, careerism, self-enrichment and violence within the ranks of the party (Southall, 2017). The manifestations of factional politics in the ANC are a key to the recent destabilisation and degeneration of this party. Such a situation aborts the historical ability of the ANC to produce leaders with integrity; who are able to rise above factional templates/ slates for a given moment for the sake of advancing genuine interests for the development and growth of the party. It is for this reason that post-1994 the ANC has produced leaders who are not ashamed to publicly declare that they "did not join struggle to be poor" (Holland, 2012). These are some of the cheap and baseless defences advanced by the leaders of the ANC post-1994 when caught engaging in corrupt activities for the sake of enriching themselves, their families and friends. The following section of the chapter situates the looming haemorrhaging of the ANC within oscillating political terrain of South Africa.

Inside the political landscape of South Africa

Unlike during the apartheid era, it has proven to be a surmounting task to rally the African masses behind the banner of the ANC. This situation can be partly attributed to the fact that in the new democratic dispensation it is not easy to identify a common enemy; and the race factor is fast becoming irrelevant in determining the outcomes of South Africa's electoral processes (Fakir & Holland, 2011). It is on this basis that traditionally white political parties such as the Democratic Alliance (DA) are now considering Blacks such as Lindiwe Mazibuko and Mmusi Maimane in their echelons. Consequently, the membership and support base of the DA is also diversified. This development contributes to the de-legitimisation of the ANC as true representative and mouthpiece of the interests of the majoritarian Black South Africans in particular and South Africans in general. The foregoing does not in any way suggests that the ANC does not have white members and supporters. The key issue is that the DA is more able to penetrate the traditional support base (Blacks) of the ANC; while the achievements of the latter to attract and retain white membership are minimal.

Contextually, the ANC appears to be failing to adapt to South Africa's changed political climate. Between the elective national conferences, succession debate in the ANC is censored. This tendency deprives the membership to know the visions of each leadership candidate; that is what they stand for in terms of the health of the ANC and the future of the country, should their election into party leadership ultimately elevate them to the country's leadership. It is on this ground that some individuals become unreliable leaders of the party and country through an accident of history. Such developments' implications pose a serious threat to the ANC and South Africa's repute in general; as evidenced in the recent era of Jacob Zuma's presidency. While it remains a key conundrum for analysts and observers in terms of what Zuma's ANC and South Africa's presidency represented; some are of the view that his lobbyists simply campaigned for him so that they can ride on his back. The conflation of the ANC's internal politics and South Africa's national politics should be understood within the context of the country's electoral system. In terms of South Africa's electoral model, the voters do not directly vote for a candidate at the provincial and national level. Instead, the voters vote for a particular political party which in turn deploys its cadres to be people's representatives in the legislature. It is for this reason that public officials (including those of the ruling ANC) tend to be accountable to their party and in a process; disloyal to the people who elected their party into power.

There is a view that the ANC is the liberator of South Africa, and therefore; most South Africans are morally obligated to vote for it. That is South Africans love the ANC and will continue to retain it in the mantle of power. This line of thought is extended by others who argue that the ANC did not only end apartheid in South Africa, but it has successfully reversed its legacy in health, education and labour sector (Shai & Ogunnubi, 2018). The combination of the aforementioned attributes should ideally contribute towards the legitimisation of the ANC-led government's rule. Regardless of the above, our position is that like ethics; morality is no sacrosanct. This is to mean that what may be viewed as morally correct for a certain group of people may not be necessarily viewed as such by others. The struggle against apartheid was not only waged by the ANC.

While the official narrative is pro-ANC, the truth of the matter is that the Pan Africanist Congress of Azania (PAC), Azanian People's Organisation (AZAPO),

Communist Party of South Africa (CPSA) and the civil society (United Democratic Front) have also contributed immensely to anti-apartheid colonial wars. Equally important, some leaders in ANC breakaway political parties such as the Economic Freedom Fighters (EFF) and the Congress of the People (COPE) have unquestionable liberation credentials which are known by all and sundry. This factor neutralises the desperate desire of the ANC to monopolise South Africa's liberation discourse as a means of entrenching its dominance on South Africa's political landscape. The argument that South Africans love the ANC may be correct but it is weak. It fails to appreciate the undisputed reality that South Africans really love basic things such as bread, land, descent jobs, adequate medical care and free quality higher education than the ANC (Mekoa, 2016). These are the empty promises that like other liberation movements in Africa, the ANC has packaged as an integral part of the anti-apartheid colonialism rhetoric (Khapoya, 2010).

These empty slogans must be understood within the context of Roger Southall's assertion that "is it is easy to criticize than to govern". The limitations on the ANC's governance of South Africa are partly because before 1990 this party did not properly prepare for the practical realities of running the country; but it was mainly focused on the immediate need of the time which was to implode apartheid. The only milestone conceivable by any measure that hinted shreds on how the ANC had sought to run South Africa was in its policy document entitled "Ready to Govern". While some of the historical promises of the ANC constituted its socialist orientated policies; it is worth noting that the forces of the neo-liberal global order have compelled the ANC to ditch them to the disappointment of the masses (Shai, 2009). This should be understood within the context that the ANC's radical and socialist orientation was diluted by the West before it came into power. For example, in the late 1980s and early 1990s the United States of America (hereafter referred to as the US) realised that apartheid was imploding and the ANC was destined to rule South Africa, Washington D.C began to court the ANC. This was a pre-emptive strategy of the US to gain influence in the future government of the ANC. It is such courtship that has enabled the US to influence the content and direction of macro-policy framework from Reconstruction and Development Programme (RDP) to Growth, Employment and Redistribution (GEAR) strategy (Shai, 2009).

Hence, when the ANC came to power, it also inherited an economy which was nearly on its knees as a result of the internationalised anti-apartheid sanctions and rampant corruption of the white minority rule under the defunct National Party (NP). For this reason, the ANC did not have a sufficient economic muscle to fund its socialist programs and which were deemed as unsustainable and not worthy of financial support by the white monopoly capital and international counterparts including Western donor countries (such Britain and the US) and international institutions such as the International Monetary Fund (IMF) and World Bank (also known as the Bretton woods institutions) (Mekoa, 2016). The influence of this donor community on the ANC and its government necessitated its shift from socialist to capitalist path. The latter was espoused through privatisation of state-owned companies (such as Telkom) whose negative repercussions became endemic under Thabo Mbeki's presidency. It is also safe to say that it is such policy shift which has served as a wedge driver between the people of South Africa and ANC under Zuma. Hence, the Zuma presidency has hopelessly failed to undo the legacy of the 1996 class project. Instead Zuma administration has nourished the legacy of the 1996 class project by producing both COPE in the year 2008 and EFF in the year 2013 and by further marginalising and weakening the South African Communist Party (SACP) and Congress of South African Trade Unions (COSATU) against popular expectations. The foregoing should be understood within the context that Zuma's administration saw and furthered the marginalisation of the left voices in the ANC led tripartite alliance.

That the tripartite alliance comprising of the ANC, SACP and COSATU was at its weakest point under Zuma's presidency is a true reflection that its leader (ANC) was degenerating or rather facing a crisis of proportions. The foregoing analysis does not suggest that Zuma is the epitome of the ANC's degeneration. In fact, even when Nelson Mandela and subsequently, Mbeki presided over the leadership of the ANC, there was already a sense that this party was on a degeneration tapestry. Thus, it was under Mandela's watch that Bantu Holomisa was expelled from the ANC. This move has provided a fertile ground for the birth of the United Democratic Movement (UDM) which was the 2nd breakaway political party from the ANC after PAC. PAC broke away from the ANC in the year 1959 due to policy differences between the moderate "charterist" and radical Africanist members of the ANC. Based on the above; it is safe to argue that the degeneration of the ANC is a historical development which was only hastened under Zuma's presidency. Offshoots from the ANC such as PAC, UDM, COPE and lately EFF, are a testament of the party that is troubled by the ghosts from its troubled past. The following section closes this chapter by advancing concluding remarks and recommendations.

Conclusion

Based on the findings of this chapter, it is clear that there is a conflation between party politics of the ANC and the national politics of South Africa. The ANC remains a dominant political party on South Africa's political landscape. But it is faced with a series of internal and external challenges that threatens its stability and the sustainability of its rule. The current ANC leadership's full ability to renew the party as a leader of South African society and arrest its degeneration is doubtful. The successor of Zuma as the President of the ANC and South Africa, Ramaphosa also subscribes to un-ANC tradition of factionalism and slate politics. As such, he is equally compromised in one way or the other. Regardless of his individual competencies, his elevation to presidency by a particular faction would render him indebted to it and this leaves him vulnerable to further manipulation by his handlers/ kingmakers at the expense of the health of the party and country at large. Last but not least, it is not farfetched that the on-going processes of self-correction on the part of the ANC lack a sense of urgency and may be too late to reclaim the lost glory of the once mighty congress movement.

References

Asante, M.K. 1990. Kemet, Afrocentricity and Knowledge. Trenton: Africa World Press.

Asante, M.K. 2003. Afrocentricity: The Theory of Social Change. Chicago: African American Images.

Burke, P. (ed.) 1991. New Perspectives on Historical Writing. Cambridge/ Oxford: Polity Press/ Blackwell Publishers.

Buthelezi, M. 2015. Debunking the myth that orality trumps literacy in Africa. http://www.polity.org.za/article/debunking-the-myth-that-orality-trumps-literacy-in-africa-2015-10-09 (Accessed 09 October 2015).

Chilisa, B. 2012. Indigenous Research Methodologies. Los Angeles: SAGE Publications.

Fakir, E. & Holland, W. 2011. Changing voting patterns. Journal of Public Administration, 46 (3.1): 1139-1152.

Holland, H. 2012. ANC grows older but not wiser. *The Star*, http://www.iol.co.za/ the-star/anc-grows-older-but-not-wiser-1207056 (Accessed 3 January 2012).

Horvath, J. 2014. Critical discourse analysis of Obama's political discourse. http:// www.pulib.sk/elpub2/FF/Ferencik2/pdf_doc/6.pdf (Accessed 02 September 2014).

Isike, C. & Ogunnubi, O. 2017. The discordant soft power tunes of South Africa's withdrawal from the ICC. Politikon: South African Journal of Political Studies, 16 (10), DOI: 10.1080/02589346.2017.1274085.

Jackson, R. & Sorensen, G. 2003. Introduction to International Relations: Theories and Approaches. New York: Oxford University Press.

Khapoya, V.B. 2010. The African Experience-An Introduction. New York: Longman.

Leedy, P.D. & Ormrod, J.E. 2013. Practical Research: Planning and Design. Boston: Pearson.

Lushaba L.S. 2016. Who am I? I am of those whose skin colour is evidence of their moral depravity, cultural decrepitly, and sexual permissiveness. I am of those on whose brown bodies modern rational knowledge has inscribed marks of inferiority, intellectual incapability and lack in all its forms. An Open letter to Professor Anthony Butler: HOD Politics Department, 30 August.

Lynch, M. 2007. Discourse analysis. In: Outhwaite, W. & Turner, S.P. (eds). The SAGE Handbook of Social Science Methodology. Los Angeles: Sage

Publications.

Mabelebele, J.M. 2008. (Dis)continuities of cultural values of black residents of Mamelodi township: Implications for public policy. Unpublished PhD thesis. Sovenga: University of Limpopo.

Maserumule, M.H. 2011. Good governance in the New Partnership for Africa's Development (NEPAD): A public administration perspective. Unpublished PhD Thesis. Pretoria: University of South Africa.

Mekoa, I. 2016. Silent No More: Challenges Facing Black African Academics at South African Universities. Cape Town: The Incwadi Press.

Modupe, D.S. 2003. The Afrocentric Philosophical Perspective: Narrative Outline. In Mazama, A. (ed.) The Afrocentric Paradigm. Trenton: Africa World Press.

Mokgosi, K.E. & Shai, K.B. 2016. Confronting the challenges and seizing opportunities for local government coalition in Gauteng Province of South Africa. Paper presented at the 5th annual SAAPAM-Limpopo Chapter Conference, The Park (Mokopane), South Africa, 26-28 October 2016.

Nkondo, M. 2012. Setting the platform for 2014 elections – Born frees learning from veterans: Talking about the future of fundamental change in South Africa. Polokwane: Electoral Commission of South Africa.

Shai, K.B. 2009. Rethinking United States-South Africa Relations. Hoedspruit: Royal B. Foundation.

Shai, K.B. 2015. How do youth movements influence parties to include youth as potential candidates on their lists and the challenges of politically aligned student's structures on campuses? Paper presented at the Independent Electoral Commission (IEC) Limpopo Provincial Youth Summit, Forever Resorts (Bela-Bela), 23-25 March 2015.

Shai, K.B. 2016. An Afrocentric Critique of the United States of America's foreign policy towards Africa: The case studies of Ghana and Tanzania, 1990-2014. Unpublished PhD Thesis. Sovenga: University of Limpopo.

Shai, K.B. 2017. South African state capture: A symbiotic affair between business and state going bad (?). Insight on Africa, 19 (1): 1-14.

Shai, K.B. & Iroanya R.O. 2014. A critical appraisal of the American ideological position on Africa's democritisation. Journal of Public Administration, 49 (3): 909-923.

Shai, K.B. & Ogunnubi, O. 2018. [South] Africa's health system and human rights: A critical African perspective. Journal of Economics and Behavioral Studies, 10 (1): 69-77.

Southall, R. 2017. The political theology of Jacob Zuma. The Conversation, http://theconversation.com/the-political-theology-of-jacob-zuma-71176 (Accessed 13 January 2017).

Van Dijk, T.A. 2001. Critical Discourse Analysis. In: Shiffrin, D. Tannen, D. & Hamilton, H.E. (eds). The Handbook of Discourse Analysis. Oxford: Blackwell Publishers.

Chapter Five

Views of profound unprecedented challenges faced by the African National Congress as a governing party by its members

Sehlare Makgetlaneng

The socio-historical background of the ANC's challenges

The ANC is facing profound unprecedented challenges in its history as a governing party. Some of its leaders and members have served as the enablers and perpetrators of 'state capture' displaying extreme arrogance and contempt for the national laws, including the constitution and the ANC positions on human rights, democracy, development and political governance conducive for their achievement and sustenance (Myburgh, 2019; Myburgh, 2017; Pauw, 2017). The acceleration of the co-option of some of its national executive leaders by the corporate finance capital 'largely explains why company owners and directors and their lawyers and accountants are so unanswerable to the government' (Orderson & Smith 2017: 23). For the first time in its history, members of the public objected to its national chairperson and some members of its National Executive Committee being on its national list to serve as Members of Parliament after 2019 elections. What led to these challenges? Their existence is recognised and admitted by its members. Some of its members provide their sources as an integral part of its efforts to confront and solve them in its quest to restore its hegemony and to serve as unassailable modern prince of the South African politics of structural social change.

This theoretical task by its members is their response to a fundamental need for a critical analysis of the challenges it faces for their concrete understanding, confrontation and resolution. Some of these challenges are consequences of its policies which have benefited its leaders, members and supporters unequally. This development has increased 'a plurality of interests and aspirations' it represents as a governing party. To best and most effectively give leadership to its increased 'diverse constituency' requires a more 'tactical flexibility and strategic vision' that call for the fundamental and structural need to successfully 'manage' these 'contradictions' (Jordan, 2012a: 9). How does the ANC ensure that an increased 'plurality of interests and aspirations' it represents is regarded as a governing party of seriousness, reliability and relevance to its leaders, members and supporters with contradictory and antagonistic interests, needs and demands is a key challenge it is facing? How should it give the best and most effective leadership to such increased 'diverse constituency' – a requisite leadership earning and sustaining respect, trust and loyalty of the members of the society is another challenge it is facing in trying to muster 'the courage for the serious introspection' for it to 'reclaim the moral high ground' (Ibid.).

The ANC through its exercise of state political power since 1994 has not adequately handled or managed these different and antagonistic needs, interests and demands. As any incomplete decolonisation is for the interests of the minority, this development is complicating its efforts in its quest for 'tactical flexibility and strategic vision' to manage the contradictions of the capitalist South Africa dominated by imperialism. Thanks to this failure, there is a consensus among the ANC members that the organisation should make strenuous efforts to have unassailable leadership quality and to heed Oliver Reginald Tambo's advice. Tambo as its 'long-serving president' whose name is 'inextricably linked' to it provided it with this leadership quality that enabled it in creating the conditions which led to its victory over the forces of the apartheid rule (Jordan 2012b: 11).

Zweledinga Pallo Jordan maintained that quality was the ANC's 'watchword under Tambo'. It executed the 'principal task' of 'knitting together a broad front of opposition to apartheid' through his 'insistence on the quality of its actions and pronouncements' (Ibid.). Its quality led it to unassailable 'measure' of its 'success.' Thanks to his 'tactical flexibility and strategic vision' required by 'a diverse constituency' he provided the ANC with under his leadership, he best and most effectively executed the task which hastened apartheid's defeat. Central to this achievement was the fact that:

> Tough, hard-nosed realism was one of his leadership skills. He understood that the oppressed people were not an uncomplicated, homogenous mass but represented a plurality of interests and aspirations that could be harnessed around the shared objective of emancipation. Giving leadership to such a diverse constituency required tactical flexibility and strategic vision that recognised the need to manage the contradictions. (Ibid.)

Tambo advised the ANC to implement requisite policies to successfully confront and solve its challenges as a governing party in his address in Angola in 1977 as follows:

> Comrades, you might think it is very difficult to wage a liberation struggle. Wait until you are in power. I might be dead by then. At that stage, you will realize that it is actually more difficult to keep the power than to wage a liberation war. People will be expecting a lot of services from you. You will have to satisfy the various demands of the masses of our people. In the process, be prepared to learn from other people's revolutions. Learn from the enemy also. The enemy is not necessarily doing everything wrongly. You may take his right tactics and use them to your advantage. At the same time, avoid repeating the enemy's mistakes. (1977)

The victory over the forces of apartheid in 1994 created contradictions which increased the ANC's 'diverse constituency' as a result of it being a governing party. This development in the history of ANC and South Africa requires a 'tactical flexibility and strategic vision' more than ever before. Very often the resolution of problems creates contradictions which require their requisite correct handling. Inability to implement decisions in handling these contradictions have led the ANC not only in failing to achieve its declared strategic objectives, but also its electoral support to substantially decline and to be defeated by the opposition in the key metros such as Tshwane, Johannesburg and Nelson Mandela Bay.

The Western powers played a crucial role in ensuring that the socio-historical injustice survived the end of the apartheid rule. Their maintenance of political and economic relations with the apartheid regime was based on their view that it was almost invulnerable to its defeat by the liberation movement. Central to their support to it were political and strategic considerations and economic factors that persuaded them to increase these relations. Increased internal opposition to the apartheid rule and the end of Angola and Mozambique as its buffer states as a result of their political independence since 1974 led the United States and Britain in particular to call for its reform. The aim of its reform was for the survival of their strategic interests in the country. In the 1980s the Western powers were impelled to conclude that political change in South Africa was necessary for their economic and strategic interests not to be 'dangerously at risk'. This was a qualitative beginning of their search for tactical means 'capable of moving South Africa in the required direction for these interests not to be changed beyond hope of repair' (Spence, 1983:502).

This position is supported by Chris Hani when in 1986 he maintained that the Western powers embarked upon this programme of action in the 1980s upon their realisation that those in power in South Africa were 'no longer able to preserve conditions of a situation where the wealth of our country is literally being siphoned out of our country'. Their 'concern' not being for 'democracy' and 'human rights', but for their 'pockets', they did 'not want to see their profits and their properties and investments going up in flames' (1986:14). They ensured the materialisation of the 'very, very important' possibility that South Africa 'should be ruled by those who are going to preserve' their 'economic interests' (Ibid.). Central to this programme of action was to ensure that the state led by the ANC was to be diverted from achieving what Frederik Van Zyl Slabbert referred to as 'popular aspirations'.

Van Zyl Slabbert and Alex Boraine established the Institute for Democracy in South Africa (IDASA) with the active support of the Western powers and organisations such as the Open Society Foundation. It became favoured recipient of foreign financial support from organisations such as the US Agency for International Development and the National Endowment for Democracy. They asked George Soros in 1987 to fund talks between the ANC and mainly white Afrikaner South African political and business leaders and scholars. The Dakar Conference in Senegal was a set of talks that contributed towards the unbanning of the ANC and other political organisations, the release of political prisoners and the negotiated settlement of the South African apartheid conflict. Before the 1987 Dakar Conference, the Open Society Foundation opened its office in Cape Town to take care of the needs of the project to ensure that the socio-historical injustice survive the end of the apartheid rule. Van Zyl Slabbert become the first chairperson of the Open Society Foundation for South Africa board.

Van Zyl Slabbert best and unapologetically articulated the objective of this project when he maintains that one of 'the most daunting challenges facing (a future government) is to protect the new political space created by negotiations from being used to contest the historical imbalances that precipitated negotiations in the first place' (1992a). In a lecture in 1992 to the South African Institute of International Affairs he pointed out that South Africans should not 'burden democracy' with 'popular aspirations'. Democracy should be saved from the 'burden' of 'popular aspirations' (1992b: 9-11) by causing divisions within the majority party including ensuring a substantial decline in its electoral support. In other words, the post-apartheid state should be prevented from achieving 'popular aspirations'. According to Ian Taylor, this is a key role that IDASA as one of 'the most active groups within the change industry' in South Africa played in 'smoothing the transition from apartheid rule' since its inception in 1987, and indeed 'the dissemination of ideology in favour of the neo-liberal project has continued unabated in the post-apartheid era. In this period, IDASA has advanced ideas that seem to propagate the notion that keeping the people away from the real levers of power i.e. the economy, is a "good thing"' (2002, 44). IDASA, supported by its donors, played a key role in infiltrating and defeating a popular movement for social justice by facilitating what Patrick Bond refers to as South Africa's elite transition which inaugurated a neo-liberal capitalist social order (2005).

The Western powers exerted pressured upon the apartheid state to execute the task ensuring that South Africa should have democracy constituting an alternative to the achievement of 'popular aspirations.' Central to this task was to see to it that the apartheid conflict was settled through negotiations while the ANC was relatively weak compared to the apartheid state. The state made strenuous efforts for the terrain of resolving this conflict to be shifted from the battlefield of mass actions and armed struggle to that of the negotiation table. F.W. de Klerk articulated this policy measure in 1991 in his declaration that:

> We did not wait until the position of power dominance turned against us before we decided to negotiate (with the ANC). The initiative is in our hands. We have the means to ensure that the process develops peacefully and in an orderly way. (in Alden 1993:71).

The ANC was not so weak during the negotiations as some of its members argue. The apartheid regime was 'meeting, steadily though stealthily, many of the preconditions' it 'set' for 'genuine negotiations' (Marais 1997:72). The target of the project of the Western powers and the apartheid regime was its view of the liberation struggle in its Strategy and Tactics. It maintained that in South Africa 'more than in any other part of the oppressed world – it is inconceivable for liberation to have meaning without a return of the wealth of the land to the people as a whole' and that it is 'therefore a fundamental feature of our strategy that victory must embrace more than formal political democracy' (in Turok 1980, 155). The point is that to 'allow the existing economic forces to retain their interests intact is to feed the root of racial supremacy and does not represent even the shadow of liberation'. This means that the struggle for 'national emancipation' is interlinked with 'economic emancipation' (Ibid., 155-56).

Pointing out that the masses of the oppressed South Africans have 'suffered more than just national humiliation'' and that the 'correction' of these 'centuries-old economic injustices' such as their being 'deprived of their due in the country's wealth', suppression of their 'skills' and their poverty and starvation' which have been their 'life experience' lies at the very core of their 'national aspirations', it concluded that 'the enormity of the problems of meeting economic needs of the mass of the oppressed people' cannot be 'effectively tackled unless the basic wealth and the basic resources are at the disposal of the people as a whole and are not manipulated by sections or individuals be they White or Black' (Ibid., 156). Briefly: 'If every racist stature were to be repealed tomorrow, leaving the economic status quo undisturbed, 'white domination' in its most essential aspects would remain' (Ibid., 141). It anticipated the reality of capitalism structurally buttressing racism in post-apartheid South Africa if it did not commit itself practically to its view of the liberation struggle.

As a result of its lack of commitment to its view of the struggle, some progressive forces, 'trade union leaders and political activists' have been incorporated into the status quo 'through enrichment once in power'. This development has 'entailed significant intellectual and political retreats and is sickeningly depressing' representing 'the minimalist imperatives of social, political and ideological containment' (Ashman, Fine & Newman 2010: 19). It has led Arundhati Roy to maintain: 'Today in South Africa, a clutch of Mercedes-driving former radicals and trade unionists rule the country. But that is more than enough to perpetuate the myth of Black liberation' (2014: 40). Rather than creating a better life for all through the structural transformation of the society, not only a rearrangement at its top, the ANC has helped to create a better life for the minority who are able to afford it.

The ANC's view of its challenges through its members

As an attempt to explain reasons why the ANC has not practically demonstrated commitment to its 'economic emancipation' agenda, this following section provides three broad views of its challenges by its members.

The attribution of the ANC's challenges to Thabo Mbeki and Jacob Zuma

Some ANC members such as Oyama Mabandla and Ben Turok attribute challenges the organisation is facing to Thabo Mbeki and Jacob Zuma. Mabandla maintains that the ANC as 'the new' organisation politically, economically and ideologically emerged after 1996 under the leadership of Mbeki. This is during the time, as he argues, that while Mandela 'reigned, Mbeki increasingly ruled'. It was during this time that it began to have a 'different mission' and 'lost its way' (2012, 13). Tenets and values that defined it under the leadership of Tambo and Nelson Mandela were replaced by 'feral and venal egos, driven by parvenus whose raison d'etre' was 'capturing the ANC for the sole purpose of personal enrichment'. He argued that 'the new ANC now genuflects and goose-steps to the siren song, 'It is our time to eat' (Ibid.). Pointing out that this 'debasement' was acknowledged by the ANC itself, he maintained that it was laid bare in 'the last six public reports by its secretaries-general' Kgalema Motlanthe and Gwede Mantashe, going back to its 51st Stellenbosch National Conference held on 16-20 December 2002. 'But, bizarrely', it 'seems supine and paralytic in decisively combating this epidemic, which is laying a waste' to its 'moral edifice' during the time it was a 'proud organisation'.

Mabandla maintains that the ANC's new 'mission' was 'the exercise of state political power and building a new nation, with all the attendant pitfalls that state power entails' and that its 'embrace of 'empowerism' or its 'location at the core' of its "new identity' was 'the proximate cause' of its 'moral implosion'. This development in its history structurally initiated 'a new zeitgeist' within the organisation and 'society at large - the deification of moolah, with being rich supplanting liberation as the leitmotif and gospel of the new South Africa'. In the process, it was 'pivoted from being a party of liberation, service and personal sacrifice to a locus for the coining of millionaires and billionaires' (Ibid.). According to Mabandla, the combination of 'liberation politics with the quest for material success was spurred further by the state's tender programme'. As a result of this programme which became 'manifestly political and grotesquely corrupt', the ANC became 'a theatre of tender wars, a prize to be captured if you wanted to get rich' quickly. He argued: 'Consumed and buffeted by this ritualistic tender cannibalism, and caught between and betwixt the logic and dialectic of empowerism', the ANC 'lost its way'. It ceased being a 'gallant movement' (Ibid.).

The Black Economic Empowerment policy driven under the leadership of Mbeki aimed at the deracialisation of the economy and the creation of the patriotic bourgeoisie has been 'something totally' not salutary. Its result has been the transformation of the 'beloved ANC into a vehicle for rapacious material accumulation' (Ibid). It has neither 'remotely succeeded in deracialising the economy nor in creating a self-sustaining black entrepreneurial class that is not dependent on the state'. It has 'most lamentably, deformed the ANC'. In his severe criticism of the ANC, Mabandla maintained that:

> But what has been most insidious about the ANC 's involvement in the doling out of BEE spoils has been its effect on the black professional class. Because the ANC has arrogated to itself the role of choosing winners and losers in this BEE game, black professionals who are dependent

on this policy for their advancement have been effectively muzzled for fear of offending the ANC and thus affecting their life chances. This has lobotomised this nation, creating a soulless society of sycophants and zombies who fear being vocal about anything that could be remotely construed as critical of the ANC fairy godmother. (Ibid)

Pointing out: 'Untrammelled intellectual discourse is a hallmark of every free and successful nation' and that a 'political culture that emasculated debate can lead only to atrophy and degeneration in the long run', Mabandla concluded that:

Criticism and intellectual dissent can only make the ANC better and our country stronger. But if the party can censure and punish those who dissent by blocking them from business deals, board appointments and executive roles in state enterprises, then the party is killing the possibility of a dynamic society. (Ibid.)

Mabandla argued that 'the new ANC' has been 'progressively debased by power, corruption, tribal atavism and intellectual vacuity' (Ibid.).

The position that that it was under the leadership of Mbeki that the ANC 'lost its direction' is also maintained by Ben Turok (2014, 75). He argues that Mbeki structurally mobilised ANC members to elect Zuma as the ANC president at its 52nd National Conference at the University of Limpopo in Polokwane, Limpopo in December 2007. According to him, the conference delegates said that they were 'fed up with his arrogance, his intolerance of dissent, and the failures of service delivery' by his administration and 'the loud support for Zuma was actually an anti-Mbeki demonstration' (Ibid., 94). Directly related to these two issues is his estimation that 'the average age of delegates' was about 38 years. For him, this means that they were 'products of Bantu Education, without the skills needed to rise in the state system or private sector. Political freedom had not brought them much improvement in socio-economic terms' (Ibid.). He supports Mabandla's position that Mbeki did not tolerate criticism and dissent. Comparing Zuma with Mbeki as the ANC president and the head of the national executive on this issue, he maintains that:

I have to concede that, whatever reservations I have about Zuma as head of the ANC and government, he has been far more permissive about diversity of views and the right to freedom of expression within the party and the administration. What is more, all who come into contact with him affirm that he is a patient listener and polite to those who differ with him. This is in sharp contrast to Mbeki. (Ibid., 96)

Cyril Ramaphosa, as the president of the ANC and the country, attributes the ANC's challenges to Zuma by arguing that it 'lost' its 'way' because of him as its president and the national president. He maintains that public institutions whose aim is to combat corruption were weakened during his administration. Without mentioning Zuma by name, he referred to his term as the period in which the state and the governing party started 'losing our way'. He was addressing residents of Lower South Coast in southern KwaZulu-Natal where he assured them that his administration is against corruption and that those engaged in it are going to be imprisoned for their corrupt activities: 'We are now on the march to tackle corruption. Those that are corrupt among us are being rooted out and they are going to go exactly where they belong' (in Goba 2019a: 4). Speaking at Marburg Secondary School on 7 January 2019, he told the residents that during the Zuma administration, the public institutions were weakened:

> In the past nine years, we started losing our way, corruption started settling in, we started weakening our institutions, or government processes started weakening.

> But fortunately, before we could go over the precipice, we realised that we have to wake up and pull the country back. (Ibid.)

Without mentioning the ANC's 54th National Elective Conference at Nasrec in Johannesburg in December 2017 by name, Ramaphosa said that the leadership that was elected at it restored hope for the country: 'I can definitely say to you, a year ago, we pulled this country back from the precipice and now we on the firm path moving forward as South Africa' (Ibid.). In his address at the Moses Mabhida Stadium in Durban on 12 January 2019, he acknowledged governance, social service delivery and corruption problems the ANC faced:

> We must acknowledge that state capture and corruption have weakened several of our public institutions, undermined effective governance and contributed to the poor performance of our economy.

> We must also acknowledge that factionalism and patronage has diminished the ability of the ANC to lead the process of transformation and fulfil its mandate to the people. (in Goba 2019b: 4)

The attribution to the ANC's challenges by its members to either Mbeki or Zuma is the secondary issue. The primary issue is their agreement that the organisation lost its historical 'direction' under their respective leadership.

Rather than the ANC losing its 'way' or 'direction' under the leadership of Mbeki as its members such as Mabandla and Turok maintain and under the leadership of Zuma as Ramaphosa maintains, the ANC's challenges intensified and became more open for them to be increasingly criticised by its members during their administrations. Mabandla's position that the ANC was captured to facilitate 'rapacious material accumulation' or 'personal enrichment' is important in that this development made what is referred to as state capture possible. It does not help in understanding sources of its challenges.

Charles Nqakula in his book, The People's War: Reflections of an ANC Cadre (2017), answers the question as to what led to the ANC's challenges. This is the question 'asked whenever small groups of serious ANC members meet and try to assess the political damage that has been caused to the movement over more than 20 years of freedom' (Sunday Independent 2017, 9). His answer to this question is that 'we walked away when wrongdoing took root and its putrid smell permeated all our hands and noses clean. We are to blame as much as the current leadership are' (Ibid.). His position that it is not only Mbeki and Zuma as individual national and ANC presidents who should be blamed for the damage caused to the organisation is of vital importance in understanding sources of its challenges and in solving them.

The ANC's challenges are not only political and economic, but also ideological or theoretical. Some ANC members articulate incorrect positions in their efforts to contribute towards solution to its challenges through their explanation and understanding. This means that its challenges are also its ideological or intellectual crises. In arguing that the ANC's problems lay in drifting away from its founding principles and practices, Nqakula draws on Pixley ka Isaka Seme's 1906 work, *The Regeneration of Africa*, which he maintains that it sets "high morality and deep-seated humanity" as the ANC's primary objectives. He concludes that:

> When the founders established the ANC, they never thought it would one day degenerate to the level where it finds itself today – penetrated by members who are bent only on financial gain and ready to use crooked means to get their hands on it (Ibid.).

His conclusion is incorrect. If, in fact, it is true that the founders of the ANC 'never thought it would one day' be characterised by problems it is facing, this raises serious questions about their quality in ensuring that that it should not drift away from its principles and practices in its struggle to achieve its strategic objectives. Any serious leadership of the liberation movement should have a room for the possibility of the organisation drifting away from its principles and practices so that when issues, processes and developments unfold threatening the materialisation of this possibility, its leaders and members would act in its best interest for it to achieve its objectives. According to Nqakula's view, Africans who established the ANC did not have a room for this possibility and strategy and tactics to ensure that it did not materialise.

The position that Mbeki and Zuma respectively made the ANC to lose its 'direction' or 'way' camouflages and hides its challenges and weaknesses which emerged before Mbeki became its deputy president and president and of the country. It is a profound theoretical misunderstanding of the political, economic and ideological challenges faced by the ANC and a failure to provide their critical analysis as a means to solve them. By shifting the blame from Mbeki to Zuma, Ramaphosa's position basically disputes this view. He articulated this blame game as the collective not absolving other ANC leaders who served in the Zuma administration, including himself from 'weakening' public 'institutions' and 'government processes'. This is understandable given the fact that he was the deputy president of the ANC and the country when Zuma was their president. As the thesis obsessing the people with their political leaders, it makes them more difficult for them to hold them accountable. It amounts to the glorification of leaders. It structurally serves leaders not the people. It structurally makes it difficult for the people to take matters into their hands in solving their national problems. As articulated by leaders, it is a self-serving view used to absolve themselves of responsibility they shouldered either being part of the problem or not taking a clear position on issues, processes and developments so as to confront challenges for their resolution.

The thesis that the ANC lost its 'direction' or 'way' because of Zuma as maintained by some of its leaders, including Ramaphosa has no logical basis. The ANC spent time, energy and resources defending Zuma when he was called upon to step down as the president. Some ANC officials including all its top six members used their power and authority in trying to keep the lid on the state capture process until it exploded beyond their control.

Mondli Gungubele, as the ANC Member of Parliament and member of the ANC Gauteng provincial executive committee, articulated the position totally different from that of the decisive majority of the ANC leaders. He called upon Zuma to step down as the national president with dignity. Central to his call was his position that ANC Members of Parliament should put the interests of the country first when they vote in the motion of no confidence in Zuma in Parliament and that he would vote against Zuma when it was tabled before Parliament. Pointing out that it was the ANC tradition to put the interests of the country ahead of the party, he concluded that when the ANC was 'born' in 1912, it was because of 'the situation in South Africa, not because of the situation in the ANC' and that the 'conduct of the ANC under the leadership of our forebears always resonated with the problems of society' (Letsoalo, 2017: 14). He added that it was wrong for the ANC leadership to threaten the party's deployees in Parliament should they not vote against the motion and that to threaten them is a sign of not 'mature democracy' for "the advancement of interests of the people' (Ibid.).

According to him, the major challenge when the motion of no confidence against Zuma was tabled was not about the Democratic Alliance or the Economic Freedom Fighters (EFF) and should be dictated by the relevance of the issue not by them. Emphasising that the ANC should 'deal with issues, not with individuals', Gungubule pointed out that Tambo as the ANC president said in 1984 at the Solomon Mahlangu Freedom College in Tanzania that 'let us tell the truth at all times even if the truth coincides with the stance of our opponents'. He further pointed out that Tambo said:

> "You cannot sacrifice the truth because it is being articulated by your enemy. For instance, if the EFF says there is a sewage leakage, are you going to say it is not leaking because so says the EFF? It is that kind of question that our movement will have to address on the day of the no-confidence motion." (Ibid.)

Gungubele's position criticising the ANC National Executive Committee for failing to hold Zuma accountable was a substantial and welcome addition to the task of saving the ANC by its leadership. Its leadership implemented its decision not to execute this task. Despite the fact that it was already too late that the ANC's reputation was already damaged, the decisive action by its leadership to say in no uncertain terms to Zuma and his supporters that the ANC is more important than Zuma and themselves and that it is serving the South African people and their country not its leaders should have made a profound difference towards repairing this damage.

Vishnu Padaachee, Robbie van Niekerk, Khulu Mbatha and Zweledinga Pallo Jordan in their works on the challenges faced by the ANC before Mbeki and Zuma became its deputy presidents and presidents respectively dispute the view that they led it in losing its 'direction' or 'way'.

The attribution of the ANC's challenges to its shortcomings and mistakes in exile

Khulu Mbatha in his book in which he attempts to unmask why the ANC failed to govern South Africa in the best interest of the majority of its people discusses its socio-economic policy thinking behind its decisions, particularly about the economy in its political strategy which led to the content of post-apartheid era. He maintains that why it is true that the ANC 'never found its feet' after 1994 is that it was 'only ready to negotiate, not to govern' (2017, 3-4). Even its 'readiness to negotiate' was 'punctuated by conspicuous shortcomings' (Ibid., 4). Despite its enormous 'political ammunition to lead the negotiations to free South Africa from apartheid', it had 'no blueprint for building a new society out of the rubble left behind'. The consequence was that it was 'vulnerable from the day the new flag was raised over the Union Buildings'. It has not solved this problem of its lack of reliable policy on issues to be able to govern the country satisfying the basic needs of the majority of South Africans. In his words:

> Even today the ANC has no reliable policy in almost all strategic areas, from the development of the economy and its essential infrastructures to education, health and science. To take this country forward the ANC relies heavily on short-term solutions or - to a large extent – on obsolete doctrines that were advanced during the time when it was still a liberation movement (a fetish that the ANC refuses to drop) and in exile. So, no policy conference is likely to deliver different results. This is the main reason why the National Development Plan is not helpful to the ANC's efforts in government. (Ibid.).

According to him, its national policy conferences held since its unbanning were not adequate in providing it with reliable policies that would have enabled it to be the best, effective, efficient, responsible and progressive political administrator of the South African society:

> All the policy conferences held so far – from 'Ready to Govern' in 1992 up to the national policy conference of June 2012 – have been inadequate to arm the ANC with the policies that would have made it a better and more modern party, able to fulfil its mandate to govern responsibly and in an accountable fashion. These policy conferences were meant to be incisive meetings but have turned out to be routine events, thus making it easy for the ANC to be captured by forces other than those wanting to

improve the lives of the people. (Ibid., 3)

According to Mbatha, the ANC has not substantiated its various declarations articulated in its documents in practice. Despite being 'armed with such slogans like 'creating one united, democratic, nonracial, non-sexist and prosperous South Africa' the ANC has no concrete plans for uniting all the people of South Africa to a common cause' (Ibid., 4). He supports his position that the ANC was not ready to govern in 1994 by quoting Nelson Mandela and Ramaphosa. (Ibid., 118-119). He maintains that:

> It was known that ANC cadres had no experience at all in running a government and its structures. But they could perhaps be forgiven. What was worse was that they have not even attempted to make preparations or to undergo training. They were deployed by the ANC without any semblance of a vetting process to at least ensure that - even if they were not trained and had no governing experience - they understood ANC policies and its objectives in general. Many had no idea about a 'people's representative' or 'a mandate from the people.'

> In the absence of these absolutely necessary measures it is apparent that the ANC was on the back foot from the beginning. We knew we had no relevant experience and yet we did not adequately prepare our people to take over. (Ibid., 119)

This raises the fundamental questions as to what was the ANC doing especially in the 1970s and 1980s in its preparation to be a governing party. To what extent did it use qualifications, experience and talents of South Africans as proud national asset in its governance of the society since 1994? He quotes Barry Gilder as maintaining proudly that:

> Many of us drawn into the public sector had little or no experience of governing, of managing large organisations and budgets, of the complex and incomprehensible processes and procedures were suddenly expected to follow, of the myriad laws and regulations we had to comply with, of the requirement for accountability and transparency the new democracy thrust upon us. And we were charged, by history and our own beliefs, with providing health, education, employment, welfare, services – and freedom – to the four-fifths of the population previously neglected by apartheid. (in Mbatha, 2017: 120).

South Gilder camouflages and hides the sources of the ANC's mistakes in its the provision of the South African society with direction in its internal and external relations as a governing party. South Africans, including members of the ANC and of their South African organisations were sent abroad for study in various fields or specialisations. Some worked for governments and other organisations throughout the world. Contrary to Mbatha and Gilder, problems the ANC faced were not because of alleged lack of experience. The ANC should have been using so many South Africans with qualifications, experience and talents within the ANC and other South African organisations in its governance of South Africa since 1994. Through some of its leaders and members, it has been preventing some South Africans with qualifications, experience and talents from serving their society in its internal and external relations. While the issue of experience is important, the issue of commitment to the cause is more vital in serving the country and its people. If some ANC leaders and members who played a key role in state capture were committed to serve South Africa and its people, the state should not have been 'captured'. Experience is accumulated in the process of executing tasks. Its admission in 1991: 'Mass campaigns conducted since the unbanning of the ANC have not been successful… Ordinary people, the bedrock of any revolution, are no longer the centre of our thinking' (ANC, 1991: 16) had nothing much to do with the lack of experience. If the masses of the South African people were no longer the centre of its thinking, how was it possible for it to substantiate its theoretical declaration to serve their interests and needs given the position of its National Working Committee in October 1992 regarded by Pallo Jordan as its consensus that it 'can win at the negotiating table only that it has secured through the struggle' (2017: 245).

Was the ANC's 1991 admission an articulation of its inheritance from the exile period? Mbatha provides some of the key reasons behind what he regards as the ANC's failure to govern the country. He maintains that the ANC was characterised, among others, by disregard for general membership by some of its leaders and those in charge of resources in the 1970s and 1980s. According to him, a 'big variance in living conditions had developed between the leadership and the general membership' which was 'even worse for those (mostly MK cadres) living in ANC camps'. Directly related to this problem were the 'lavish and show-off lifestyles, including the arrogant attitudes of those in leadership positions and in charge of resources'. These constituted 'a source of much frustration' on the part of the general membership. The leadership was criticised for the way they adopted and implemented policy decisions by the ANC members, including 'a substantial number of the MK cadres' who lost confidence in the leadership (2017: 45). These practices of the ANC leaders in exile and their treatment of the ANC members including those tasked with waging armed struggle as a means for it to be victorious over the apartheid state raise the fundamental question as to whether they were going to be committed in practice to the qualitative betterment of the material conditions and rights of the South African people and behave in a manner substantiating their declarations in practice since 1994. They were against the ANC's declared battle cry of the better life for all.

The ANC's 'performance in government today, which is far below expectations' is directly related to 'the shortcomings and mistakes it made in the period of exile' (Ibid., xvii). Providing some of them, he maintains that it ignored the South political economy. Although it knew its development and its dominated integration into global capitalism, it 'gravely overlooked' it to 'the extent of not discussing it at all' (Ibid., 49). It is for this reason that he calls this neglect of the requisite discussion of the South African economy 'the missing fifth pillar in the struggle against apartheid' (Ibid.). What he regards as the 'excessive concentration on the armed struggle' through which 'the question of South Africa's economy was ignored' (Ibid.) was its profound weakness on the ideological front of the struggle. One of the reasons is because armed struggle was viewed as if it was the objective to be achieved, not a means to defeat the apartheid regime politically for it to effect the socio-economic restructuring of the society. Because of these weaknesses and 'omissions', the ANC was 'left unprepared for future challenges, especially concerning the economy' (Ibid., 47-48). This made it 'weak on a very serious aspect of the liberation struggle, although previously it had always emphasised that liberation must have meaning if our people are to be economically liberated' (Ibid., 48). The consequence was its profound weakness not only on the economic front, but also on the political and ideological fronts in providing the direction to the struggle for the content of post-apartheid society.

Central to Mbatha's position that the ANC was not ready to govern the country is the question as to what extent did it substantiate its theoretical understanding in practice on the requirements of the war of the national liberation? This question is of vital importance given the fact that for the war of national liberation to be effective, sustained and successful it 'required more than simply carrying arms into the battlefield; it required more than just a determination to fight, or simply the acquisition of launching and training bases from friendly countries, or moral and material support from friends' (Murapa 1977: 11). It is guided not simply by the zeal to seize and exercise state political power but also by ideological imperatives striving to bring into existence a system of socio-political, economic and ideological justice (Ibid.).

The ANC never ruled out in principle a negotiated settlement of the apartheid conflict. Its mobilisation of support globally was to ensure that the apartheid regime was forced to the negotiating table. Despite this reality, it did not adequately prepare itself for the negotiations with the apartheid regime. Mbatha maintains that it did not take negotiations seriously. This had decisive impact on its preparations for negotiations and key issues, processes and developments related to them. In his words:

> I believe that had the issue of negotiations been taken seriously, the next question to have arisen would have been: negotiations for what? This would have finally brought the ANC to discuss the future of South Africa's economy, insofar as liberation was concerned, but because this never happened it left the organisation devoid of policy on this front and open for manipulation. (2017: 48)

Padayachee and van Niekerk support this reality when they write that the apartheid regime the ANC negotiated with was 'weakened by international sanctions and internal resistance, not to mention the psychological impact of the armed struggle' (2017: 18). They support Mbatha's position that the ANC did not take the negotiations seriously and that this had decisive impact on its use of the negotiations to achieve a common strategic goal when they maintain that:

> There is evidence that the way in which the ANC worked on policy in general was highly fragmented, compartmentalised, and to some extent personalised. Each NEC [sub]committee, including the DEP, worked in its own silo, hugely influenced by who was at the top of these committees,

and with little or no reference to what other complementary policy committees were doing, with little or no coordination from the centre driving towards a common goal, and most significantly with only very tenuous links to the formal negotiations in CODESA and the multi-party talks where key policy decisions were being approved. (Ibid., 16)

These challenges are such that the thesis that the ANC 'lost its way' or 'direction' under the leadership of Mbeki and Zuma camouflages or hides challenges it has been facing as Mbatha maintains. The fact that the socio-economic restructuring of the society is the secondary issue depending on how the assumption or seizure of state political power were prepared and is exercised supports the position that the ANC did not best and most effectively organise itself by having socio-economic policies and programmes to serve the South African people to their satisfaction.

Jordan is one of the ANC members who recognised these challenges or weaknesses and anticipated their possible negative consequences during the negotiations. He disagreed with key points of the document, Strategic Perspective, drafted by the ANC Negotiations Commission, in October 1992 in his response to Joe Slovo. It was discussed by the ANC National Working Committee (NWC) at its meeting during the last week of October in 1992. According to him, its authors elevated negotiations to the level of strategy. He pointed out that:

> The unwarranted elevation of negotiations to the ANC's primary strategy has the unfortunate outcome of re-orienting the movement away from confrontation with the enemy to a search for common ground. 'Strategic Perspective' exudes a desperation to discover such common ground at all costs. Rather than discovering ways of enhancing the growing confidence of the mass of the oppressed as the agency of their own liberation, it advises the ANC to discover a new way of facilitating communication between its leadership and the regime. Amazingly, this is seen as a 'breakthrough.' 'Breakthrough' into what? One may well ask!

> The harm this can inflict on the movement is already evidenced by the confused signals which have emanated from the NEC [National Executive Committee] – its oscillation between militancy and complacency. (2017: 244-45)

According to Jordan, they were happily ignorant of the history of the twentieth century in their document. 'To be generous', he wrote in 1992, 'the authors' of the document "appear charmingly ignorant of the history of the 20th century' (Ibid., 246). Its 'logic' fundamentally departed from the strategic objectives of the ANC (Ibid., 239). The 'national liberation of the most oppressed and exploited' was its 'central objective' (Ibid., 241). Its proposed compromises during the negotiations were bound to 'undermine' the ANC's "strategic objectives or subvert the achievement of national liberation' (Ibid., 249).

The apartheid regime's 'immediate objective was to render the ANC 'too weak to resist' its 'compromise' (Ibid., 248) for it to achieve its strategic objective to retain 'the essentials of White power – i.e. the accumulated, palpable privileges that the Whites, as a dominant racial group, enjoy in terms of ownership and control of the decisive sectors of productive property' (Ibid., 240). He concluded that:

> While quite prepared to make room for Blacks to enter the political domain, the regime is determined to so condition what power the majority acquire that it will frustrate any attempts to tamper with these essential of White power (Ibid.)

The regime had achieved its strategic objective. The beneficiaries of the apartheid rule have retained their 'accumulated, palpable privileges' as a racial group. The consequence is that they are the primary beneficiaries of the post-apartheid rule under the leadership of the ANC.

The attribution of the ANC's challenges to its neglect of economic and social policy thinking in its political strategic since its formation

Padayachee and van Niekerk maintain in their book provisionally entitled, Shadows of Liberation? ANC Economic and Social Policy from African Claims (1943) to GEAR (1996): 'Talks over the transition to democracy in South Africa began fitfully and (largely) in secret in the mid to late 1980s' (2017: 13-14). This statement is of vital importance for several reasons. Central to these reasons is the fact that the ANC had enough time to prepare itself politically, economically and ideologically as a governing party best, most effectively, efficiently and progressively in confronting problems it inherited and in solving those bound to emerge since 1994. Some scholars maintain that it did not seriously prepare itself for the execution of this political governance task. As a result of this failure, Padayachee and van Niekerk argue that twenty-five years since it became a governing party, firstly, its progress in addressing 'some of the legacies of the apartheid regime in economic and social terms' has "not been as widespread, fast or as sustainable as may have been expected for'. Secondly, unemployment, inequality and poverty problems it defines as the 'triple challenge' issues, and "the challenges of economic growth itself remains stubbornly intractable, and appears by most evidence-based research, to be getting worse in some respects'. Thirdly, 'a serious crisis of service delivery (water, sanitation, electrification, health) in many parts of the country and a concomitant rise in serviced delivery protests and labour action, and weak performance" by both 'big and small firms', a 'double whammy of macroeconomic disequilibrium and microeconomic stagnation faces the country today'. Fourthly, 'corruption, personal accumulation projects and governance challenges add to the woes of a new democracy' (Ibid., 14). They conclude that:

> A serious, sober and 'warts and all' analysis of how South Africa has reached this point is necessary and perhaps overdue. Part of the explanation for the current malaise, we maintain, lies in the historic neglect of economic and social policy thinking in ANC political strategy since its formation in 1912. (Ibid.)

As a result of the ANC's socio-historical neglect of economic and social policy thinking in its political strategy, key national and global forces and 'influences impacted' on a negotiated settlement. 'One key' national factor that emerged in this development was 'the residual power of the late apartheid regime in the arena of economic policy-making, in which the powerful and confident Derek Keys, was a central reformist figure in the part of the white minority regime' (Ibid.). They quote Ben Turok as observing with 'great insight' that:

> Although the ANC had done some work on a future programme for government in the Reconstruction and Development Programme and Ready to Govern, these were only broad policy documents. There was no plan of how an ANC government would actually take over the administration of the country, nor did it have trained personnel to run the country. Consequently, it took over most of the personnel from the apartheid regime and only replaced them incrementally in the following years. Hence the actual arrangements of transition were carried out by apartheid officials, especially in the Treasury. (in Padayachee and van Niekerk 2017a: 14)

Global forces antagonistically inimical to the declared ANC strategic objectives provided members of its Department of Economic Planning (DEP) with weapons to entrench their economic and social interests in South Africa under its political leadership. The role played by these global forces in 'the crucial years of the transition to democracy and beyond' constituted some of other negative consequences. Members of its DEP with few exceptions, (while smart and streetwise) were unevenly or inappropriately trained in economics, as well as inexperienced in economic analysis and policy formulation. Many too eagerly imbibed a few weeks of 'crash course' training in economics provided to them by the World Bank, J.P. Morgan and other corporate ideologues who had an intentional agenda of shaping in a pro-market direction policy idea, possibilities and limits of post-apartheid economic reform. (2017: 14-15)

The aim of their book is to understand 'the clearly complex and often haphazard and somewhat murky process by which decisions about economic and social policy were taken in the negotiations over a democratic constitution" and in 'the early years of democracy' (Ibid., 12). Their work represents 'an attempt to critically assess the economic and social policy theorising, thinking and choices' made by the ANC and its alliance partners in the transition to post-apartheid South Africa or from 1985 to 1996. Their periodisation starts with the African Claims document produced by the ANC under the leadership of Alfred Bitini Xuma in 1943. It ends in the publication of the Growth, Employment and Redistribution document produced by the ANC as a governing party under the leadership of Mandela. They argue that the ANC had 'a very clearly articulated social democratic agenda on a post-segregation and post-apartheid 'good society' and that this was 'specifically described' by Albert Luthuli as taking the institutional form of a 'democratic social welfare state'. In the 1940s and 1950s it had "no hesitancy in confidently locating South Africa in the global world of progressive social policy ideas" and "indigenising' them in the efforts to resolve the South

African 'national question' (Ibid., 13).

This social democratic agenda was not adopted as a well-elaborated socio-economic policy sustaining its progressive vision reflected in policy development guideline documents such as African Claims and the Freedom Charter. The consequence was the ANC leadership began to embrace development framework structurally supporting the socio-historical injustice.

They explain set events which negatively impacted on a negotiated settlement of the apartheid conflict. They are, firstly, the fact that the ANC's DEP was 'over-stretched in trying to satisfy multiple and often trivial calls' on its 'services and time'. Despite 'some initial attempts', it 'failed sufficiently to engage with its own rich mass democratic base to develop and defend its position'. This led the ANC being 'outmanoeuvred' in economic policy debates by the apartheid government and institutions which had been shifting increasingly towards a neo-liberal approach to economic policy since the early 1980s. The role of the powerful South African companies in this 'persuasion' process was not 'determining' the way 'some argue. (Ibid., 15)

Secondly, 'the fatal consequences of a weak' ANC DEP which 'in effect completely de-linked themselves from the mass democratic movement, 'going it alone' against the residual power of the old apartheid state as well as its 'well-resourced' economics institutions and personnel' was one of these processes or events. The ANC's economic policy choices in 'the mid-1990s' stemmed in their view from this 'fundamentally uneven balance of power created' (Ibid.).

They quote John Samuel who they regard as the 'hugely respected ANC educationalist and civil servant' writing in Sunday Times on 30 July 2017 on the early years of the post-apartheid government making 'a broadly similar point in a more elegant style' as maintaining that:

> Despite much preparation, we were not at all prepared for the subterranean text on the walls of the old government offices we moved into. The absence of guidelines shaped by the ideals of the struggle, coupled with pervading old apartheid culture, was a toxic mix (Ibid.).

One of the key reasons behind this lack of preparation and readiness to govern was that the ANC as compared to the apartheid regime and its institutions which were 'powerful and globally connected' with the advanced capitalist countries 'fragmented, under-resourced and under-capacitated having perhaps necessarily (and to a point understandably) 'placed all its resources into the primary objective of overthrowing an undemocratic, racist and repressive white minority regime' (Ibid., 14).

Despite the fact that when negotiations began, the ANC had enormous support among the majority of the South African people, continentally and globally and that they were its 'major assets', power did 'lay in the hands of white business and in the institutions of the … apartheid state which inevitably influenced the constituencies engaged in informal and formal negotiations' (Ibid.). Padayachee and van Niekerk quote Martin Plaut who argues: 'The men who had run South Africa for decades also embarked on a process designed to incorporate senior members of the ANC. Radical economic policies were dropped in favour of more conventional macro-economic prescriptions' (Ibid.). They maintain that one of the reasons behind this development is the fact that the ANC historically neglected 'economic and social thinking' in its 'political strategy' since its formation in 1912. It paid dearly for this omission of the execution of the task on the economic and ideological fronts of the struggle. Its profound consequence is that it was structurally not prepared on these fronts in serving its political strategy in the turning point of the history of the movement towards post-apartheid era in effecting economic restructuring of the society.

Turok maintains in 2017 that at the founding of the ANC in 1912 the dispossession or deprivation of land was 'a major issue, especially' as the Native Land Act of 1913 was coming into existence which led to 'the erosion of the basic means of production for millions of Africans'. He also maintains that:

> In the ensuing years the ANC was concerned with the loss of political and civil rights as was set out in African Claims of 1943. But there too there were a series of economic demands under the headings of land, industry and labour, and commerce. It called for "the right to an equal share in all the material resources of the country," as well as rights to own and acquire land in rural and urban areas (2017b:15).

He maintains that the Freedom Charter adopted in 1955 was a further opportunity for the ANC to have its economic policy. During this time the South African Communist Party and the labour movement forces began to advance socialist policy measures for economic change. Some ANC members opposed these measures and 'highly contested' the economic clause of the Freedom Charter. 'Remarkably', despite the fact that it contains 'radical formulations such as that the mineral wealth beneath the soil, the banks and monopoly industry be transferred to the ownership of the people as a whole', it has "never been challenged in any ANC conference' (Ibid.). He argues that, however, as the 'succeeding years were preoccupied with the concrete struggle for the liberation', these 'issues were laid aside' (Ibid.).

Acknowledging that South African major companies were willing to invest time and financial resources in initiatives so as to dissuade the ANC from embarking upon what they viewed as socialist economic programmes including nationalisation and redistribution, Padayachee and van Niekerk maintain that their research, especially interviews they conducted with Ango-American Corporation executives suggest that capital 'anticipated making concessions to the ANC's vision of redistribution to a greater degree, than it eventually turned out the ANC was willing to push for' (Ibid., 17-18). Their central position is that there was 'little willingness in the ANC leadership to exploit the political opportunity that existed in the transition era to wrest concessions from the conglomerates on the need for more fundamentally re-distributive economic policies' (Ibid., 18). How did South Africa under the leadership of the ANC fundamentally shifted away from its original vision of a just socio-economic order after victory over the apartheid rule in 1994?

Their answer to this question is that the ANC faced profound challenges upon its unbanning in operating in South Africa. They were, firstly, its continued lack of 'history or tradition' of economic theoretical work and, secondly, its lack of support from the former Soviet Union. The third challenge was the rejection of 'any substantive engagement with the alternative progressive ideas coming out' of the Reconstruction and Development Programme processes, the Macro-Economic Research Group and 'an inclusive democratic engagement on economic policy with its own internal constituency' by its 'inexperienced' DEP. The consequence was that the ANC was 'out-manoeuvred by the apartheid regime and local conglomerate capital' on socio-economic policy with the result that there was 'no need for 'secret talks' to bring this about' (Ibid).

Conclusion and recommendations

This chapter has provided analysis of the three broad views of profound unprecedented challenges faced by the ANC as a governing party by its members. The first view attributing these challenges to Mbeki and Zuma, argues that it was under their respective leadership that it lost its historical direction. This view is not helpful in understanding their sources and solution. Issues, processes and developments leading to the right of South Africa to its true national self-determination and the free, independent exercise of its sovereignty and domestic policy in the best interests of its people and for this right to be respected by its leaders should not be left into the hands of its two leaders irrespective of the unquestionable content of their commitment to the liberation struggle. Political administration of the society is the collective process in which two individuals are not indispensable. This view being personal raises key questions. What structurally prevented the ANC members from theoretically and practically committing themselves to its declared objectives and those of the country including constitutions from mobilising themselves and using their strength and resources in challenging Mbeki and Zuma as presidents of the ANC and the country as the necessary measure to have collective leadership and the democratic means capable of adequately substantiating their position on the requirements of these objectives and constitutions in practice before they were defeated at the national conferences? Why revolutionary and progressive forces within ANC did not democratically fight against those theirs was hostility to the new leadership of the party and the country as required by the situation – the struggle fought for under the pretext of defending the unity of the party? This view is not helpful in answering these questions. It is not in the interest of the country and its people in defending the unity of the party if its president is against the popular national interests. The unity of the national liberation movement in power cannot seriously depend on the power and authority of one person.

An answer to these questions is, among others, well-entrenched dependence on the ANC by its leaders and members as well as some black and white businesspersons. This is one of its key challenges bound to increase its internal divisions and tensions and, in the process, complicating its renewal agenda. Its renewal agenda is bound to be made more difficult by the results of investigations into corruption activities involving its leaders and members as well as some black and white businesspersons. Its challenges are bound to get worse before they are resolved.

The second view attributing its challenges to its shortcomings and mistakes it made in exile raise issues in essence articulated in the third view arguing that the ANC's challenges are a result of its historical neglect of economic and social policy thinking in its political strategy since its formation. While they are useful in understanding shortcomings and mistakes made by the ANC in the strategic area of socio-economic policy, it is not sufficient in explaining why the ANC has continued since 1994 not seriously advancing the interests of the majority of South Africa and in facing its challenges. As maintained by Padayachee and van Niekerk it is extremely economistic view devoid of the acknowledgement of the strategic importance of political factors central of which is the commitment to the cause. The ANC's lack of history or tradition of economic policy theoretical work cannot seriously be regarded as the key reasons behind challenges it is currently facing. To the extent that its challenges are more political relating to leadership and governance crises not so much economic crises is such that political issues have been having primacy over economic issues. While appropriate economic policy is important, it is the broad capacity to govern characterised by the ability to project state power on the basis of independent legislature and judiciary holding the executive accountable in its protection of the citizens through the creation and sustenance of the conducive conditions for them to have better, safe living and working conditions. Without these progressive and capable administrative requirements for the exercise of freedom by the citizens in having active say in how they are governed and who govern them and ensuring that they are provided with equitably public goods, a governing party with the appropriate economic policies on issues may not progressively serve the people.

The ANC members whose views of the organisation's challenges are analysed in this work do not discuss the role of the Western powers in these problems. This is their profound weakness and omission. This factor applies to works of some scholars on the Southern African liberation movements in power (Southall, 2013), the South African revolution (Saul, 2013) and crises (Ashman, Fine & Newman, 2010; Hart, 2013) 'authoritarianism in Africa' (Moore 2015) and edited book volumes on the position of Mbeki on South Africa's internal and external relations (Glaser, 2010; Jacobs & Calland, 2002). It applies also to a proliferation of magazines in South Africa declaring to be progressive such as Amandla! This theoretical task amounts hiding plans of the Western powers in their strategies and tactics in preserving and expanding their continued control and exploitation of Southern Africa's resources.

Despite the role played by advanced capitalist countries in establishing and maintaining relations of inequalities, domination and exploitation with Southern Africa, the relationship between them and the regional countries is primarily not the external process. It is primarily the internal process. Southern Africa's regional situation should be analysed by taking into consideration primarily dynamics of its specific internal movement which determines it. Key socio-political and economic factors within Southern Africa determine the consequences of the international situation upon its national situation. Discussion and explanation of the challenges faced the Southern African liberation movements should include the relationship between the region and Western powers for their concrete understanding. As an integral component parts of global capitalist order, the internal situation of Southern Africa and their governing parties cannot be adequately and fully analysed in isolation from this social order. This theoretical task should be executed and achieved on the basis of the dialectical, concrete historical and class analysis of its specific or particular national situation without losing sight of what is taking place externally throughout the world particularly within international capitalism.

The ANC's challenges include its failure to prepare for and manage the transition. It behaved and acted as if it was fighting only the apartheid regime not also Western powers serving as its senior allies. Given this failure, it did not have strategies and tactics to deal with the forces of imperialism in a country which is relatively more developed than any other African country. Southern Africa under the leadership of South Africa occupies a key strategic position in the plans of the Western powers for their continued control and exploitation of Africa's resources. The Western powers used any means necessary including dividing some ANC leaders and members and compromising them and infiltrating it to ensure that South Africa does not serve as the structural obstacle towards their continued control and exploitation of its resources and those of the region and continent. This struggle continues. The ANC has paid dearly for not seriously recognising this programme of action and confronting it for its defeat especially within itself.

The ANC's profound ideological challenge is that it did not lay the foundations of economic emancipation during the course to end the apartheid rule. Its two-stage theory made it difficult if not impossible to execute this task. It should serve as a clear and unambiguous forward movement towards the resolution of the articulated and combined misfortunes of capitalism and racism that are in the form of persistent poverty and lack of socio-economic security for the decisive majority of South Africans. Without this, it would leave more South Africans with no other alternative but to join opposition political parties in increasing its pain or loss of support and further visualising the country being not under its leadership. It should demonstrate in theory and practice that it is addressed by the socio-economic problems faced by the majority of South Africans by using its exercise of state political power to act as their unassailable collective intellectual in their efforts to create their own better life. Directly related to this demonstration of commitment to think and act in the interest of those who have been regarding it as their organisational servant, it should ensure that South Africans who live in relative comfort and security contribute towards the resolution of socio-economic problems their fellow nationals face. This may mean the ANC transforming itself from being a broad church of members with different and antagonistic positions on issues, processes and developments into a cohesive organisation with direction guided by political, economic and ideological imperatives in rendering this service to the country and its people.

Notes

J.E. Spence reviewed two books dealing with political developments in Southern Africa and the efforts by independent countries of Southern Africa towards their economic liberation which required Western powers to change their policy towards the apartheid regime for the survival of their strategic interests in South Africa in post-apartheid era. On these issues, refer to Barber, Blumenfeld & Hill (1982) and Nsekela (1981).

References

African National Congress. 1991. Mayibuye: Journal of the African National Congress, October: 15-18.

Alden, C. From liberation movement to political party: ANC foreign policy in transition. South African Journal of International Affairs, 1(1): 62-81.

Ashman, S., Fine, B. & Newman, S. 2010. The crisis in South Africa: Neoliberalism, financialization and uneven and combined development. In: Panitch, L., Albo, G. & Chibber, V. (eds). The Crisis This Time: Socialist Register 2011. New York: Monthly Review Press.

Barber, J., Blumenfeld, J. & Hill, C. R. 1982. The West and South Africa. London: Routledge and Kegan Paul.

Bond, P. 2005. Elite Transition: From Apartheid to Neoliberalism in South Africa. Pietermaritzburg: University of KwaZulu-Natal Press.

Glaser, D. 2010. Mbeki and After: Reflections on the Legacy of Thabo Mbeki. Johannesburg: Wits University Press.

Goba, N. 2019 Party admits to mistakes made. Sowetan (Johannesburg), 14 January: 4.

Goba, N. 2019. Ramaphosa says ANC had lost its way under JZ.' Sowetan (Johannesburg), 8 January: 4.

Gungubele, M. 2017. In Matuma Letsoalo. 'Vote for the country, not the party', Mail & Guardian (Johannesburg), May 5 to 11: 14.

Hani, C. 1986. 25 years of Armed Struggle: Army Commissar Speaks. Sechaba, December: 14-15.

Hart, G. 2013. Rethinking the South African Crisis: Nationalism, Populism, Hegemony. Pietermaritzburg: University of KwaZulu-Natal Press.

Jacobs, S. & Calland, R. 2002. Thabo Mbeki: The Politics and Ideology of the South African President. Pietermaritzburg: University of Natal Press.

Jordan, Z.P. 2017. Letters to my Comrades: Interventions and Excursions. Auckland Park: Jacana Media.

Jordan, Z.P. 2012a. Does ANC have the courage for introspection? Business Day (Johannesburg), 13 December: 9.

Jordan, Z.P. 2012b. Quality was the ANC's watchword under Tambo. Business Day (Johannesburg), 25 October 2012: 11.

Mabandla, O. 2012. Eat, drink and be very afraid. Sunday Independent (Johannesburg), 21 October: 13.

Marais, H. 1997. South Africa, Limits to Change: The Political Economy of Transition. New York and Cape Town: Zed Press.

Mbatha, K. 2017. Unmasked: Why the ANC failed to Govern. Sandton: KMM Review Publishing Company.

Moore, D. 2015. An arc of authoritarianism in Africa: Toward the end of a liberal democratic dream?' In: Panitch, L. & Albo. G. (eds). The Politics of the Right: Socialist Register 2016. New York: Monthly Review Press.

Murapa, R. 1977. The leadership struggle in Zimbabwe: Background. First World: An International Journal of Black Thought 1(1): 1-51.

Myburgh, P. 2017. The Republic of Gupta: A Story of State Capture. Cape Town: Penguin Random House.

Myburgh, P. 2019. Gangster State: Unravelling of Ace Magushule's Web of State Capture. Cape Town: Penguin Random House.

Nsekela, A.J. 1981. Southern Africa: Towards Economic Liberation. London: Rex Collins.

Nqakula, C. 2017. The People's War: Reflections of an ANC Cadre. Johannesburg: Mutloatse Arts Heritage Trust.

Nqakula, C. 2017. Political damage obvious in the ANC. Sunday Independent (Johannesburg), 18 June: 9.

Orderson, C. & Smith, P. 2017. Who runs South Africa? The Africa Report (Paris) 88: 23-31.

Padayachee, V. & van Niekerk, R. 2017. 'Shadows of liberation': Economic and social policy from African claims to GEAR'. New Agenda: South African Journal of Social and Economic Policy 67: 12-18.

Pauw, J. 2017. The President's Keepers: Those Keeping Zuma in Power and out of Prison. Cape Town: Tafelberg.

Roy, A. 2014. Capitalism: A Ghost Story. London: Verso.

Saul, J.S. 2013. On taming a revolution: The South African case'. In: Panitch, L., Albo, G. and Chibber, V. (eds). The Question of Strategy: Socialist Register. New York: Monthly Review Press: 212-35.

Southall, R. 2013. Liberation Movements in Power: Party & State in Southern Africa. Pietermaritzburg: University of KwaZulu-Natal Press.

Spence, J.E. 1983. Review of two books. Third World Quarterly 5(2): 502-04.

Tambo, O. R. 1977. OR Tambo speaking at the Mkhonto we Sizwe military camp in Angola in 1977.

Taylor, I. 2002. South Africa's transition to democracy and the 'change industry': A case study of IDASA.' Politikon: South African Journal of Political Studies 29(1): 31-48.

Turok, B. 2017b. Nothing much has changed. The Star (Johannesburg), 30 June: 15.

Turok, B. 2014. With My Head above the Parapet: An Insider Account of the ANC in Power. Auckland Park, Johannesburg: Jacana Media.

Turok, B. 1980. Strategy and tactics of the African National Congress. In: Turok, B. (ed.) Revolutionary Thought in the 20th Century. London: Zed Press.

Van Zyl Slabbert, F. 1992a. The Quest for Democracy: South Africa in Transition. London: Penguin Books.

Van Zyl Slabbert, F. 1992b. The Burden of Democracy. Johannesburg: South African Institute of International Affairs: 1-13.

Chapter Six

Jacob Zuma-led ANC as a home of major contradictions

Kgothatso Shai

Introduction and Background

This chapter seeks to employ the Afrocentric perspective as an alternative theoretical lens to analyse the pre-2018 major political and ideological contradictions in the ANC within the context of its intersection with the government. This is because most of the works on this discourse have been framed from a North[ern] angled view, which only provides a partial understanding to African political institutions such as the ANC and its government (Mashele, 2017). The year 2009 is used as a starting point for this chapter because it served as a watershed moment that ushered the inauguration of Jacob Zuma as the president of South Africa. This chapter ends in 2018 because it was in this year that President Zuma resigned as the president of South Africa. The period between the year 2009 and 2018 is arbitrarily considered by the author of this chapter as adequate for generating a crispy understanding of the major political and ideological contradictions in the ANC; but to also draw lessons for like-minded political institutions in Africa (Shai & Molapo, 2017).

Contextually, it was on the 31st March 2017 that South Africa and the international community was awakened by breaking news of the 8th cabinet reshuffle to be implemented by President Zuma since he assumed Pretoria's (administrative capital of South Africa) mantle of power during the year 2009. It is instructive for the reader to bear in mind that Zuma has succeeded Thabo Mbeki as the President of the ANC following the latter's 52nd elective conference in Polokwane (administrative capital of the Limpopo Province of South Africa) during December 2007. It is also worth noting that the elevation of Zuma to the most senior executive position in the national leadership of the ANC has paved a way for him to succeed Kgalema Motlanthe as the President of South Africa. While Zuma stayed as the President of the ANC from the year 2007 to 2017, his political party deputy (Motlanthe) had served as a caretaker President of South Africa following the resignation of Mbeki from the highest office in the land in September 2008 (Chikane, 2012). The circumstances which led to Mbeki's resignation as the President of South Africa are beyond the scope of this chapter. It suffices to mention in passing that he did not voluntarily resign from his position per se.

But it was a resolution and/or instruction by the National Executive Committee (NEC) of the ANC for him to do so. These developments were precipitated by spurious allegations that Mbeki has previously abused state institutions to fight intra-party battles. Inasmuch as it was unconstitutional for the NEC to force Mbeki to resign as the state President, the latter tendered his resignation due to his well-considered understanding that he was serving in that capacity on the behest of the ruling ANC (Republic of South Africa, 1996). The foregoing should be understood within the context that the current electoral model of South Africa is based on political parties. This is to mean that public representatives at national and provincial levels generally are not directly elected by the people. Instead the electorate vote for political parties. Based on the number of votes that each party acquire during elections, it is then able to deploy representatives using the Proportional Representation (PR) system (Vuma, Raphala & Shai, 2016).

The evolving public discourse on the real motive behind the March 2017 cabinet reshuffle is polarised; and it necessitates a deeper reflection on some of the political and ideological contradictions facing the ANC. According to then President Zuma the March 2017 round of cabinet reshuffle was driven by the desire to promote efficiency and effectiveness in service delivery (Manyathela, 2017). This standpoint is questionable especially if one is to consider the fact that such critical decisions in respect of the deployment of public representatives in the mode of ministers and their deputies was traditionally done in consultation with the ruling ANC. This does not in any way take away the President's constitutional prerogative to hire and fire ministers (Republic of South Africa, 1996). But it is the entrenched tradition of the ANC; that is in appreciation of the fact that whoever the President of the country becomes does not emerge on his individual capacity but under the ticket of the party that won elections (Vuma, Raphala & Shai, 2016). This is a similar principle that was previously applied in arriving at the decision to remove Mbeki as the President of South Africa.

Three of the top six (6) officials of the ANC, namely then Deputy President Cyril Ramaphosa, Secretary General Gwede Mantashe and Treasurer General Zweli Mkhize publicly made a pronouncement on their displeasure about the overhaul of the cabinet (Hunter, Jika & Mokone, 2017). The shared views of these three (3) officials are that except in the case of the former Finance Minister Pravin Gordhan, they were not adequately consulted about other changes to cabinet. In reaction to what was purported as consultation; this group argued that it was not a *de facto* consultation. But it was more of an announcement of a list of changes prepared elsewhere. The foregoing interpretation should be understood within the context that the secretive and combative manner in which Zuma handled the aforementioned cabinet reshuffle lend credence to allegations of state capture (Shai 2017a). This insinuation has been central to the strengthened resurgence of the #ZumaMustFall movement during the year 2017. While Ramaphosa, Mantashe and Mkhize have since apologised for publicly distancing themselves from such cabinet reshuffle; the important thing to note is that such pretentious apology would not bury the realities of on-going tensions within the leadership ranks of the ANC. It was just a hypocritical show of unity which fits into nothing but a cheap public relations exercise by the degenerating ANC (Shai, 2017b).

Emphatically, this chapter is largely underpinned by the theory of Afrocentricity as articulated by scholars such as Asante (2003) and Chilisa (2012), among others. It also draws from the works of Modupe (2003) and Maserumule (2011). Unlike the Westernised theoretical perspectives which are dominant in the social sciences and other knowledge faculties, the author of this chapter has found and chosen Afrocentricity as its theoretical lens due to its ability to generate and project knowledge from an African perspective. It is asserted that Afrocentricity is introduced in this chapter since it has an intellectual sanctuary for the other knowledge systems (i.e. African) which are dismissive of the binary logic of knowledge production (i.e. as empirical or non-empirical; subjective or objective; good or evil) (Asante, 2003; Chilisa, 2012; Maserumule, 2011). The triangulation of written data on the political history of the ANC and the author's personal experience on the practice of South African politics seeks to show that the written text and the subjective knowledge are not linear and there is a long-standing close relationship between them (Burke, 1990; Buthelezi, 2015).

The interface between ANC protocol and constitutional prescripts of South Africa

It is argued that there are serious tensions that characterise the interaction between the ANC and government. This is especially the case when it comes to the question of the composition of the faces of government. By and large, the key challenge facing the ANC is the lack of consistency in the application of its principles and standards for defining and constituting leadership. For example, in the year 2008 the NEC of the ANC was in agreement in its successful effort to force Mbeki to step down as the President of South Africa. Inasmuch as there was a dominant perception, allegations and *prima facie* evidence that Mbeki had abused his state power to fight internal party battles, he was neither charged nor found guilty by the court of law. In contrast, Zuma was faced with close to 800 charges of corruption before he became the President of the ANC in year 2007 and subsequently of the country in the year 2009. These charges were dropped by the erstwhile National Director of Public Prosecutions (NDPP) Mokotedi Mpshe under controversial circumstances; which were seen as a broader plan to clear any hurdles on the bumpy road towards Zuma's return to the Union Building (administrative hub of the South African government).

To make matters worse, the year 2016 witnessed the Constitutional Court of South Africa delivering a unanimous judgement that has found that Zuma has broken his oath of office thereby failing to protect and defend the constitution of the Republic of South Africa, Act 108 of 1996 (Shai, 2017a). Regardless of this and other decisions by then President Zuma that threatened the very sustainability of the ANC as the ruling party in the country and future of South Africa's political and economic stability; the proposed move to remove Zuma as the President of the country was not fathomable but it latter happened in February 2018. Hence, there are influential personalities within and beyond the ANC who were of the view that Zuma must finish his term of office as the President of both the party and country at all costs. For example, the other two (2) top officials of the NEC, namely: then National Chairperson Baleka Mbete and Deputy Secretary General Jessie Duarte were in agreement that then President Zuma should finish his term of office at the party and governmental level. Collen Maile, the president of the African National Congress Youth League (ANCYL) and Bathabile Dlamini, the then president of the African National Congress Women's League (ANCWL) also shared this view. This view was also stretched far by the erstwhile Transport Minister Joe Maswanganyi who has vociferously argued that those who are against Zuma's cabinet reshuffle were basically implying that the country should have "a lame duck' president who is not allowed to discharge his mandate" (Tandwa, 2017).

The politics of the stomach as captured by Manyaka (2016) and Mathekga (2017), and the phenomenon of "arranged leadership" as articulated by Motlanthe captures the essence of the rejection of #Zuma must fall campaign in certain circles (Madisa, 2017). Such rejection was not underpinned by anything close to the interests of the ANC and the national interests of South Africa. Regardless of the series of scandals that have plagued Zuma's administration, it was apparently difficult for the NEC of the ANC to remove him as the President of the ANC and/or South Africa because he still enjoyed solid support of the ANCWL and ANCYL. This is the type of political structural support that Mbeki did not have during the time of his fall (Mathekga, 2016). Unlike in the case of Zuma, it was easy for the NEC to remove Mbeki as the state President because he was already ousted as the President of the ruling ANC. It is for this reason that it became plausible for the ANC to recall Zuma as the country's President in February 2018 because his political base was eroded as a result of the change of party leadership in December 2018.

Meanwhile, there is no sound basis to believe Zuma's assertion that the March 2017 cabinet reshuffle was about fostering of efficiency and effectiveness in service delivery. Hence, the erstwhile political head of national treasury, Gordhan along with his then deputy Jonas Mcebisi were some of the best performing ministers before they were reshuffled in March 2017. For example, Gordhan and Mcebisi have spearheaded efforts to restore investor confidence on South Africa and ultimately risked the country's economy from falling into a junk status as a result of the controversial circumstances surrounding the substitution of well-known Nhlahla Nene with Des van Royen at the helm of treasury during December 2015 (Shai, 2017a). Among those that have been reshuffled during March 2017 is Ngoako Ramatlhodi (ex-minister of Public Service and Administration), Dipuo Peters (ex-minister of Transport) and Derek Hanekom (ex-minister of Tourism). While the performance of this three (3) was not outstanding; but they were certainly better than some of the ministers who have been retained in the cabinet and subsequently, redeployed to other portfolios by then President Zuma.

In contrast, there were ministers such as Bathabile Dlamini, Faith Muthambi and Malusi Gigaba whose performance in cabinet left much do be desired. It is common knowledge among South Africans that Dlamini has openly and deliberated disobeyed the rule of law thereby not meeting deadlines in terms of following proper procurement processes to find a replacement company for assuming the responsibility of the disbursement of social grants from Cash Paymaster Services (CPS). This failure to observe the rule of law until the last moment when CPS's contract was about to elapse left the government with no choice but to extend the contract of CPS against the earlier wishes of the court of law. It is no exaggeration that social security scheme's beneficiaries were only able to receive their grants on the 1st April 2017 not through the competence of Dlamini; but through the intervention of the court of law. It is also no exaggeration that the failure by Dlamini to give proper leadership and guidance on the issue under consideration had created a confusion and uncertainty among most of the beneficiaries of the social grants. Despite this, she was retained as the minister of Social Development by Zuma until she was redeployed to the Department of Presidency in February 2018 by the new President.

In the same breath, Gigaba has presided over the erosion of corporate governance in the majority of state-owned enterprises (SOEs) such as Electricity Supply Commission of South Africa (ESKOM) and Passenger and Rail Agency of South Africa (PRASA) during his term of office as the minister of Public Enterprises (Derby, 2017a). Before he was elevated to Treasury, he was serving as a minister of Home Affairs under which he presided over the introduction of controversial rules about visas. It goes without saying that the introduction of controversial visa rules by Gigaba led Home Affairs Department has dampened the performance of the tourism industry, one of the mainstays of South Africa's economy. To add to this list, I can add Muthambi who presided over the fast-tracked degeneration of South African Broadcasting Corporation (SABC) in her capacity as the former Minister of Communications (Manyathela, 2017).

Based on the above exposition, it is safe to argue that then President Zuma's narrative over the synergy between the cabinet reshuffle and service delivery is full of lies and reminiscence of the abuse of power. There is logic in one believing that the March 2017 round of cabinet reshuffle was driven by three main reasons. Firstly, it was about removing ministers who were opposed to then Zuma and by extension his ex-wife, Nkosazana Dlamini Zuma. It must be recalled that in the past, Derek Hanekom had proposed a vote of no confidence in Zuma in one of the NEC meetings. During the run up to the December 2017 ANC elective congress the drastic action for removing deviant ministers was important for paving a way for Dlamini-Zuma to become the President of the party and possibly, that of South Africa. Inasmuch as Dlamini-Zuma and Zuma have divorced, there is mutual sympathy and trust between them which is anchored on the fact that they have children together.

Logically speaking, Dlamini-Zuma would not want to see corruption charges faced by the father of her children in the past being reinstated and ultimately, putting him at the serious risk of being imprisoned. To this end, it becomes very crucial for Zuma to reward people who have identified themselves with his ex-wife's campaign to become the President of the ANC and subsequently, South Africa. The latter was not necessarily automatic. It is dependent on the outcome of the 2019 general elections in South Africa and the performance of the ANC in this regard. In the same line of thought, those who were against such a campaign ought to have been removed and retain those who supported the presidential candidate that is fully trusted by Zuma. The foregoing analysis dovetails with the survival of the Dlamini as the Minister of Social Development, in spite of her dismal performance. It is notable that not axing Dlamini shows how Zuma desperately wanted his ex-wife to take the presidential seat. Hence, Dlamini-led ANCWL had already endorsed Dlamini- Zuma's candidature to become the ANC President after the 54th national elective conference that was held in December 2017.

Secondly, the March 2017 cabinet reshuffle was about the entrenchment of the parasitic patronage network of Zuma's family and friends, particularly the Gupta family. The foregoing should be understood within the context that the two chief victims of the cabinet shuffle had not made it easy for Zuma and Gupta families to individually and jointly loot the state coffers. For example, Mcebisi has been in the forefront in terms of revealing damning allegations of state capture by the Gupta family and for him to be continuously retained in the cabinet partly emboldens those who are anti-Zuma (Shai, 2017a). Furthermore, Gordhan have had legal battles with the Gupta family. Against the latter's wish and non-expressed sympathy by Zuma, Gordhan have made it clear that it is not his responsibility to force relations between the Gupta owned Oakbay Investments and major South African banks. Major South African banks have closed bank accounts owned by Oakbay Investments and its subsidiaries following damning allegations of state capture. Major South African banks who have severed their business ties with the Gupta owned Oakbay Investments and its subsidiaries include Amalgamated Banks of South Africa (ABSA), First National Bank (FNB) and Standard Bank. Equally important, Gordhan has stopped the move by Zuma and Gupta families to complete the agenda for capturing the South African treasury for the sole benefit of their business enterprises (Mthombothi, 2017). Key among the items frustrated by Gordhan was his refusal to approve the trillion-rand nuclear deal with Russia which stood to mainly benefit the Gupta and Zuma family. While the Zuma led ANC claimed to be against corruption and other evil activities that eat away from people-centred development, the reality on the ground suggested the sense of self entitlement by then dominant faction in the Zuma led ANC that it is its "time to eat" (Shai & Rankhumise, 2007; Derby, 2017b).

Thirdly and lastly, there is a narration that is based on baseless intelligence report. This narration says that Zuma recalled Gordhan and Mcebisi from his cabinet because they have been cited in an intelligence report to be collaborating with foreign markets and banks, and international rating agencies to undermine Zuma's authority and ultimately, bring about regime change in South Africa (Hunter, 2017). This narration has not been publicly confirmed by then President Zuma. However, it was claimed by the South African Communist Party (SACP) that Zuma has cited issues pertaining to the intelligence report in question among the reasons for the reshuffle of the Finance ministry. That it is not clear as to whether the source of this intelligence report is the domestic intelligence community or foreign intelligence service casts aspersions on its credibility. The lack of credibility on the report of this nature renders it unsound to make major governance decisions on their basis. When Mbeki was still a President there was once an intelligence report of this mode. In the Browse Mole Intelligence Report Zuma was accused to be conniving and getting financial support from Angola to dislodge Mbeki from power.

At that time, no one has ever acted individually or collectively in view of persecuting Zuma on the basis of baseless intelligence report. If it is true that Zuma was influenced to reshuffle cabinet by the intelligence report in question, it then becomes paradoxical for him to act against his fellow comrades like Gordhan on the basis of shoddy intelligence report. It is the well-considered view of this chapter that it was unwarranted to recall Gordhan and Mcebisi from the recent overseas investment promotion road show and subsequently, remove them from cabinet. This chapter contends that a combination of Gordhan and Mcebisi struggle credentials and commitment to clean government exonerate them from any possibility of engaging in unpatriotic actions that may bring about an externally brewed regime change (Hunter, Jika & Mokone, 2017).

The central theme of President Zuma state of the nation address (SONA) on the occasion of the official opening of parliament for the year 2017 was radical economic transformation. For some observers, radical economic transformation is an empty rhetoric meant to reclaim the lost electoral fortunes of the ANC during the 2016 local government elections. It is also understood in certain circles that majority of South Africans are not pleased with the pace of service delivery and transformation of economic structure of South Africa. After more than two (2) decades of majority rule since the first general, democratic and inclusive elections in 1994, the colonial patterns of the South African economy remain intact. This argument is advanced by other observers who argue that it is wrong to even begin to talk about radicalising something that has never worked in South Africa such as economic transformation (Friedman, 2017). Following this rhetoric on radical economic transformation which left the spines of the investor community shivering, then Finance Minister Pravin Gordhan later contained the situation by assuring those frightened that the fiscal policy of the country will stay the same. But the first press conference of Gigaba as the Minister of Finance reflected that there is political will to change the fiscal policy of this country (Skiti, 2017). His views were more in line with those expressed by the president on radical economic transformation. In other words, Gigaba's views were a total anti-thesis of the stand used by Gordhan to allay fears of the investors. Whether the views of Gigaba would have had a substantive effect on the fiscal policy direction of this country is neither here or there. The key issue is that it is important to carefully tread on the perceptions of the investor community because such has a potential to influence investment direction.

There is sense among some analysts that it was within the rights of Zuma to remove Gordhan and Mcebisi from cabinet because the duo's relationship with the President was on the rocks. However, this position was rejected by the SACP. SACP had argued that Zuma and Gordhan do not have to be personal friends (News24Wire 2017). It is further argued by this party that Zuma and Gordhan are comrades and ought to rise beyond personal feelings/ preferences and put the interests of the country first. The foregoing argument has elements of truth but it stops short of appreciating the fact that the empty perceptual space between professionalism and personality does not exist in the realm of practice.

In the same breath and following the March 2017 (in the middle of the night/ witch-hour) cabinet reshuffle, the Congress of South African Trade Unions (COSATU) also registered its worries due the reality of misperceptions and misunderstandings between the ANC and its allied partners, SACP and COSATU. COSATU was extremely concerned that then President Zuma had for the first time taken a decision to change his cabinet without consulting it. It is not surprising for COSATU to have expectations to be consulted because it has consistently and regularly supported the ANC during elections since the year 1994. It was also sensible for COSATU to make this observable abnormally on the part of the President's decision making in the re-composition of his cabinet. Hence, one of the reasons why both COSATU and SACP had actively campaigned for Zuma to replace Mbeki as the President of the ANC during the year 2007 was due to the shared belief among them that Mbeki administration had marginalised them in decision making within government circles (Mathekga, 2016; Shai, 2016b). This marginalisation is not something that they thought will be perpetuated by President Zuma. What can be deduced from the assertions of some of the prominent leaders of the ANC-led tripartite alliance is that the March 2017 cabinet reshuffle was implemented in a divisive and factionalist fashion. The emergence of this alien and unaccountable form of ruler-ship in the ANC as represented by then President Zuma is cancerous to the much-needed unity for the survival of the party and tripartite alliance as a whole.

To compound matters to an already worst situation, the March 2017 cabinet reshuffle had a clear potential of reviving tribalist and racist tendencies; a precedent that is totally against the fundamental values of the ANC. It would appear that Zulu cadres of the ANC have benefited more than any other group out of the changes in the national executive of the government in March 2017 and many others presided by then President Zuma (Mthombothi, 2017). That then President Zuma is a Zulu partly explains the revitalisation of this very dangerous and often downplayed tribal factor in the politics of the ANC and South Africa as a whole. Nonetheless, I am of the view that Zuma is not necessarily tribalist. But his decisions were more about resource control by a particular identical group; which turns out to be dominated by Zulus.

Conclusion

Based on the findings of this chapter, it can be concluded that the Zuma led ANC was indeed a home of major political and ideological contradictions.

These contradictions can be observed when located in both historicity and contemporaneity. During Zuma's presidency of both the ANC and government, there were deep-seated disagreements among the leaders of the tripartite alliance about questions of the composition of ANC leadership and by extension, deployment in government circles. Lies, double speak and also abuse of state power fist into the disagreement among the leaders and constituent parts of the tripartite alliance. At the centre of the political and ideological fissures that characterised the ANC-led tripartite alliance during the period under review, was the lack of clarity and focus on the content and direction of the fiscal and/or economic policy of South Africa as advanced by the ANC. As such, the ANC seemed not to have the capacity for redemption; amicable and irrevocable resolution of its contradictions. This is an unfortunate situation that serves as time bomb for the party to degenerate further and ultimately, preside over a doomed political and economic future of the country like any typical African state that obtained majority rule before South Africa.

Considering that the ANC is the oldest liberation movement in Africa, it is crucial for likeminded formations in the continent to draw lessons from its experiences in the government of South Africa. Equally important, other governing parties should strive to avoid ANC's sins of incumbency as reflected in its major political and ideological contradictions; for the purpose of maintaining their power or regaining their lost political ground.

References

Asante, M.K. 2003. Afrocentricity: The Theory of Social Change. Chicago: African American Images.

Burke, P. (ed.) 1991. New Perspectives on Historical Writing. Cambridge/Oxford: Polity Press/ Blackwell Publishers.

Buthelezi, M. 2015. Debunking the myth that orality trumps literacy in Africa. http://www.polity.org.za/article/debunking-the-myth-that-orality-trumps-literacy-in-africa-2015-10-09 (Accessed 09 October 2015).

Chikane, F. 2012. Eight Days in September: The Removal of Thabo Mbeki. Johannesburg: Picador Africa.

Chilisa, B. 2012. Indigenous Research Methodologies. Los Angeles: SAGE Publications.

Derby, R. 2017a. Ex-ANC youth boss switched loyalty from Mbeki to Zuma. Sunday Times, 2 April 2017.

Derby, R. 2017b. As new gang takes over, let's hope Gigaba's fidgeting days are over. Sunday Times, 2 April 2017.

Friedman, S. 2017. Radical economic transformation: Why it's nothing to fear – Steven Friendman, *BizNews*. http://www.biznews.com/leadership/2017/02/16/radical-economic-transformation-steven-friedman/ (Accessed 16 February 2017).

Hunter, Q. 2017. Surprise! How No. 1 broke news to reshuffled staff. Sunday Times, 2 April 2017.

Hunter, Q., Jika, T. & Mokone, T. 2017. It's open revolt: Top ANC leaders break ranks as president's midnight cabinet purge brings internal conflict to a head. Sunday Times, 2 April 2017.

Madisa, K. 2017. ANC doesn't want members to vote because they want arranged leadership: Kgalema Motlanthe, Sowetan. http://www.sowetanlive.co.za/news/2017/02/28/anc-doesn-t-want-members-to-vote-because-they-want-arranged-leadership-kgalema-motlanthe (28 April 2017).

Manyaka, R.K. 2016. Zuma and the politics of the stomach, *Politicsweb*. http://politicsweb.co.za/opinion/zuma-and-the-politicsofthestomach (Accessed 25 February 2016).

Manyathela, C. 2017. Zuma: Cabinet reshuffle to improve efficiency and effectiveness, *Eyewitness News*. http://ewn.co.za/2017/03/31/zuma-says-reshuffled-cabinet-to-improve-efficiency-and-effectiveness (Accessed 31 March 2017).

Maserumule, M.H. 2011. Good governance in the New Partnership for Africa's Development (NEPAD): A public administration perspective. Unpublished PhD Thesis. Pretoria: University of South Africa.

Mashele, P. 2016. South Africa is just another African country – tell the 'clever blacks', *BizNews*. http://www.biznews.com/africa/2016/12/22/south-africa-will-finally-be-an-african-country/ (Accessed 22 December 2016).

Mathekga, R. 2016. When Zuma Goes. Cape Town: Tafelberg.

Mathekga, R. 2017. South Africa, you are on your own against Zuma. Sunday Times, 2 April 2017.

Modupe, D.S. 2003. The Afrocentric philosophical perspective: Narrative outline In: Mazama, A. (ed.) The Afrocentric Paradigm. Trenton: Africa World Press.

Mthombothi, B. 2017. Gordhan the real target; the others were collateral damage. Sunday Times, 2 April.

News24Wire. 2017. SACP rubbishes Zuma's claims about Gordhan's road show. http://www.polity.org.za/article/sacp-rubbishes-zumas-claims-about-gordhans-road-show-2017-03-30 (Accessed 30 March 2017).

Republic of South Africa. 1996. The Constitution, Act 108 of 1996. Pretoria:

Government Printer.

Shai, K.B. & Rankhumise S.P. 2007. Reflections on the state of human security in the aftermath of the February 2007 elections in Lesotho. *Inside AISA*, Policy Brief, July.

Shai, K.B. 2017a. South African state capture: A symbiotic affair between business and state going bad(?). *Insight on Africa*, 9 (1): 62-75.

Shai, K.B. 2017b. Afrocentric appraisal of ANC under Jacob Zuma: An age of [de]generation? Paper presented during the Colloquium on Liberation History, Memory and Contestation co-hosted by the National Institute of Humanities and Social Sciences (NIHSS), Universities of Venda, Limpopo, Zululand and South Africa, Thohoyandou, 15 - 17 March 2017.

Shai, K.B. & Molapo R. R. 2017. The "decriminalisation" of the# FeesMustfall movement in South Africa: An Asantean perspective. Commonwealth Youth and Development, 15 (1): 1-16.

Skiti, S. 2017. New finance minister talks tough on SOEs. Sunday Times, 2 April.

Tandwa, L. 2017. We won't allow Zuma to 'be treated like a lame duck' - new transport minister, *news24*. http://www.news24.com/SouthAfrica/ News/we-wont-allow-zuma-to-be-treated-like-a-lame-duck-new-transport-minister-20170403 (Accessed 03 April 2017).

Vuma, S.L., Raphala, M.G. & Shai, K.B. 2016. South Africa's 2016 municipal election campaign: An Afrocentric critical analysis. Paper presented at the 5th annual South African Association of Public Administration and Management (SAAPAM)-Limpopo Chapter Conference, The Park (Mokopane), South Africa, 26-28 October 2016.

Chapter Seven

The ANC's Christianity-driven morality as political theology through the X-ray of Ahmed Kathrada

Kgothatso Shai

Introduction

Since the Roman Empire (27 BC-476 AD), relations between the church and the state has always been a hotbed for thinkers and practitioners operating in either politics, religion or both (du Plessis, 2017). The discourse in this regard is deeply divided. For instance, there is currently an unpopular view that the church should be actively involved in politics for the purpose of serving as a torchbearer and advocate of God's laws within the political and government circles (ACDP 2019). This view is unpopular because it enjoys the support of the few in contrast to the majority who oppose it by virtue of understanding that the societal roles of the church and political parties should not be blurred (West, 2019). Most Christians consider the church as their spiritual home and the very same segment of the population have parties that they regard as their political homes; by virtue of being their members, supporters and/or sympathisers (Crafford, 1993). This unpopular view is also contested by those, like Julius Malema of the Economic Freedom Fighters, who believe that the church is too holy to be entangled in the "dirty business" (Morgenthau, 1948) of politics.

Despite these polarised views, history is littered with evidence attesting to the constructive role of churches and religious leaders in mapping the political agenda and future of many countries, including South Africa (Shai & Mothibi, 2015; Pityana, 2018). For example, it is common knowledge that during the struggle against apartheid in South Africa, some churches provided hide-outs and safe nests for a number of political activists and members of liberation movements such as the ANC, Pan-Africanist Congress of Azania (PAC) and Azanian People's Organisation (AZAPO) (West, 2019). Archbishop Desmond Tutu, Reverends Alan Boesak and Frank Chikane are some of the prominent names of local men of the cloth who were in the forefront of the struggle against the inhumane and brutal apartheid system (Venter, 2017). In fact, Tutu, Boesak and Chikane were instrumental in globalising the anti-apartheid struggle by establishing and maintaining solidarity networks with international partners. While the liberation movements were banned in South Africa and their leaders exiled, these leaders engineered anti-apartheid community-wide mass mobilisations under the auspices of the United Democratic Front (UDF) (Molapo, 2005).

In the post-apartheid era, some churches provided shelter to some of the victims of the 2008 xenophobic attacks in South Africa (Shai & Mothibi, 2015). This political engagement is in the same mode as the church's engagement with the anti-apartheid struggle. It should be understood that during the apartheid era, progressive churches served as safe havens for political activists, whose lives were endangered by the violence unleashed in the townships by South Africa's security establishment (Mzala, undated). Despite the notable and constructive roles of the church in our political landscape, there is a feeling in certain circles that the church's moderate and non-violent approach has somehow derailed the processes that led to the end of apartheid in the early 1990s. This view is aggravated by the fact that the Holy Bible was exploited by the architects of apartheid to justify white minority rule (Farisani, 2014; West, 2019). The non-violent nature of the groups led by Tutu and Boesak is well captured in Venter's (2017: x) account of the protest against the September 1989 whites-only election when she noted that "[o]ur pain turned to joy when in their outrage, and led by Archbishop Desmond Tutu and Reverend Alan Boesak, thousands of people crammed the streets of Cape Town in a peace march". Regardless of the competing opinions about the need for the church's involvement in politics, it is not uncommon to see the articulation of theological expressions by ANC leaders for the purpose of mobilising their members, supporters, and sympathisers to rally behind a particular political cause (Beyers, 2015).

While the submission that theological expressions by ANC leaders qualify as political theology is debatable, when looked at systematically and in an integrated form, they can be equated to guiding theological principles of the party. The influence of religious (Christian) ANC leaders on the party's activities and how such is perceived by the ordinary people cannot be under-estimated. Although not expressed in the official policies of the ANC, the manner in which the political morality of its leaders is normally judged cannot be easily divorced from political theology, particularly Christian doctrines. It is within this context that this chapter attempts to discuss the meaning and essence of the ANC's Christian morality as political theology in the post-apartheid era. To realise this, the author heavily depends on the wisdom of a late stalwart of the ANC, Armed Kathrada, as recorded in Sahm Venter's (2017) *Conversations with a Gentle Soul*. Kathrada's experiences, opinions and encounters are used to formulate systematic views about the political theology of the ANC. This is because the life and times of Kathrada were shaped by the ANC in several ways and his wisdom cannot be wholly delinked from the collective wisdom of the ANC (Chetty, 2018). This approach is feasible if one is to consider the fact that history is broadly considered as the laboratory of Political Science (Shai, Molapo & Sodi, 2017; Asante, 2003). The foregoing assertion also dovetails with Ayanda Dlodlo, the then Minister of the South African Department of Public Service and Administration's invocation about the role of veterans (including those of the ANC) in the quest to transfer knowledge from one generation to the other (Pretoria East Rekord, 2018).

Political theology, Afrocentricity, and methodological considerations in perspective

The conceptualisation of concepts in the Social Sciences and Humanities is a contested terrain (Rankhumise, Shai & Maphunye, 2008). In this chapter, political theology is understood as political culture about the [ab]use of theological principles and values to justify a particular political conduct (Van Wyk, 2015). In this context, political theology also denotes a resort to Christian values, scriptures, and dictates by the ANC during the different stages of South Africa's political history. It is worth noting that in practice, the ANC is a multi-faith political party dominated by Christians. Even those members of the ANC and South African citizens who practice African traditional religion largely submit to Christian values as and when it is convenient for them (e.g. during burials). While there are differences between Christianity and the other religions practiced in South Africa, commonalities can also be observed. For example, all religions in South Africa renounce violence.

The dominance of Christians and their values in the ANC captures the national religious dynamics of South Africa. But deviation from such theoretically and rhetorically embraced religious doctrines is not uncommon. Regardless of one's moral standing, such conduct may either be good or bad (Raphala & Shai, 2016). In recognition of the reality that the correctness of the labelling of one conduct as either good or bad is dependent on social context (Maserumule, 2011), the author has opted to locate this chapter within the Afrocentric theory and paradigm (also read as Afrocentricity). As articulated by Asante (2003), Afrocentricity was chosen as a contextual and theoretical lens for this chapter due to its functional and cognitive role. A quick review of the literature on the subject of this chapter shows that the few related studies that have been conducted in this regard were largely done from a Eurocentric perspective (Mazama, 2003). The foregoing assertion should be understood within the context that the provincialisation and colonisation of academic disciplines such as Political Science and Theology is a Western construct (Ndlovu-Gatsheni, 2018).

For this reason, efforts to realise epistemic justice naturally demand that historically marginalised concepts, theories, and philosophies from Africa, by Africans, and for Africans, such as Afrocentricity, should be used to operationalise the research for chapters of this nature (Maserumule, 2015). At the heart of Afrocentricity is the claim that the knowledge of reality about African phenomena (the political theology and morality of the ANC in this case) can be well generated when studies about them are underpinned by African value systems, standards, and tools (Asante, 1990). In terms of political theology/morality and in general, African value systems entail peace, cooperation, interdependence, and communalism, inter alia (Mazama, 2003). If Africa (inclusive of South Africa) is considered as the cradle of humankind, then Africa is also a cradle of all world religions, including Christianity, Buddhism, and Islam (Naidu, 2008). It would appear that all of these religions emanated from African traditional religion. As and when they deviated from the fundamental principles of African traditional religion, alien tendencies/practices were built into them.

It is instructive to note the following tenets of Afrocentricity as pioneered by Modupe (2003), which are invoked as the analytical categories of this chapter:

- Grounding is the process of learning that is centred on the Africans, their, history, culture and continent.

- Orientation "is having and pursuing intellectual interest in the African and the formation of a psychological identity direction, based upon that interest, in the direction toward Africa".

- Perspective denotes self-awareness of viewing and affecting the world in a manner that prioritise the African interests and which is suggestive of the quality, kind and amount of the above-mentioned two elements.

Any radical deviation from this prescription constitutes what is termed a "transversal error". The foregoing observation is not necessarily dismissive of the utility or value of theories and concepts imbued in Western value systems in helping us understand political and theological issues in Africa. The point here is that the universalisation and violent imposition of Western concepts and theories is ill-conceived by any measure (Shai, Nyawasha & Ndaguba, 2018). Given that like systems, theories and concepts borrow from one another for the purposes of self-enhancement, it then becomes feasible and fair to accord Afrocentricity an equal status with its Western counterparts in order to allow for the germination of fresh and alternative truths to orthodox accounts (Asante, 2003).

This chapter also draws from some of the fundamental features of discourse analysis as outlined by Van Dijk (2001):

- It must be better than other studies in order to gain recognition.

- It must be centred on social and political issues, rather than current paradigms.

- Explains discourse structures in terms of properties of social interaction.

- The primary focus is on the ways discourse structures enact, confirm, reproduce, or challenge relations of power and dominance in society.

These features are relevant to this chapter because it heavily depends on document study and content analysis of the speeches of ANC national leaders. This approach is particularly useful for researching this descriptive chapter which deliberately avoided interviews due to time and resource constraints.

Hatred and bitterness reconsidered in context

According to Venter (2017), historic accounts show that negative emotions such as hatred and bitterness did not hang on to Kathrada. Considering that Kathrada's generation was influential in formulating the historic culture of the ANC, it is not an exaggeration to argue that before 1994, hatred and bitterness did not find expression in the life and blood of the ANC (Chetty, 2018). It is within this context that Kathrada's close comrade and friend, Nelson Mandela, once averred that:

> No one is born hating another because of the colour of skin … people must learn to hate, and if they can learn to hate then they can be taught love, for love comes more naturally to the human heart.

This powerful political statement can be closely linked to the biblical commandment: "Thou shalt love thy neighbour as thyself" (Matthews 22: 39 as cited in Bible Gateway 2018). If post-1994 relations between ANC members are anything to go by, one can say that members of the different factions within the party hate each other more than they hate members of the opposition parties (Manyathela, 2018). This is reflective of the extent to which factionalism, regional cleavages, and careerism have consumed the moral fibre and organisational discipline of the ANC (Shai, Ndaguba & Nyawasha, 2018; Nyawasha, 2018).

The foregoing analysis can be rejected as a simple "gamble", an assumption that the differences between party members which lead to factionalism are underpinned by hate. Such an assumption is true to a certain extent but cannot be generalised. This is because studies of factionalism within parties show that amongst others, these differences are driven more by internal struggles for power, positions, privileges, alignment with particular policy stances, and divisive leadership within the party rather than hate for each other (Nyawasha, 2018; Bujra, 2019). These manifestations have had spill over effects to the extent that post-1994 political conduct is in contradistinction with the founding values of the political theology and morality of the ANC, which is largely immersed in Christianity (Crafford, 1993). Due to the influence of the West on the knowledge structure of the political economy of South Africa, non-Christian views have not found notable expression in the national debates that are often led by ANC national leaders. This does not in any way suggest that Muslims, Buddhists, and others cannot be found in the ANC, but it reflects their position's margination in national political and theological discourses. The foregoing analysis should be understood within the context that the first set of meetings towards the establishment of the precursor of the ANC, the South African Native National Congress (SANNC), in 1912 were largely attended by pastors, chiefs, and people's representatives, *inter alia* (Saunders, 2012).

Venter (2017) points out that in the 1950s, Kathrada engineered the disruption of the meeting of IB Tabata of the Non-European Unity Movement through the use of gangsters. The motive behind this somewhat act of political intolerance and ill-discipline was driven by Kathrada's and the collective's desperate desire to contain the encroachment of the Non-European Unity Movement in Johannesburg, an area that was largely deemed as the territory of the ANC. Regardless of the motive behind the disruption, the key issue is that the renting of criminal elements for the sake of carrying out a political mission is questionable by any moral standard. What can be drawn from the foregoing analysis is the imperfection of Kathrada and his generation; a characteristic that invalidates their fronting like saints. These imperfections can also be observed in the contemporary social milieu of the ANC (Modjadji, 2018).

The ANC's theological-political rhetoric in perspective

While rendering the eulogy to the late Nelson Mandela, Kathrada, as cited in Venter (2017) said:

> We are a country that has been blessed by many great and remarkable men and women, all of whom have played a critical role in the liberation of our country. We have been blessed by the contribution of the many different movements and formations, both inside and outside the country, who stood by us in the dark days of apartheid.

He then zoomed this narrative into the ANC, acknowledging its embracing the clause in the Freedom Charter which reads that "South Africa belongs to all who live in it". These highlighted parts of Kathrada's speech are in contradistinction of the populist rhetoric of former President Zuma and his political cronies that "the ANC will rule until Jesus Christ comes" (Koko, 2017). These extracts also show that unlike the current crop of national leaders, populism was never a defining characteristic of the fathers of South Africa's democracy. Thus, it is safe to state that Kathrada's generation never had an appetite for scoring cheap political points through the advancement of a piece-meal or biased historical narrative of the liberation struggle. This situation can be attributed to the fact that age and time never favoured them to the point of suffering from the ANC's sins of incumbency (Seale, 2017) thereby avoiding the tendency to re-write history through the terms of reference that are pro- the seating government. The use of historical re-writes to achieve short-term political goals has proven to be a major weakness of most seating governments and governing parties around the globe. However, Kathrada's generation fully appreciated the reality that depending on the will of the majority, every South African citizen or political party is eligible to rule South Africa (Republic of South Africa, 1996).

It is common knowledge that Jesus Christ is dead and, scientifically, cannot resurrect. Taking a cue from this, the insinuation that "ANC will rule until Jesus Christ comes" suggests that this party will govern South Africa until eternity. This argument is misleading if the recent declining electoral fortunes of the ANC in three metropolitan municipalities (Tshwane, Johannesburg and Nelson Mandela) are anything to go by (Mokgosi, Shai & Ogunnubi, 2017). We learn that Kathrada's generation appreciated time keeping. Using the wisdom of Kathrada's generation to predict the future, it is not too farfetched to assume that the noble loss of electoral support in the urban areas by the ANC signifies that the end of its rulership of South Africa is near. This interpretation bears similarity with the ancient prophetic writing about Nebuchadnezzar's kingdom in ancient Babylon as captured in the bible (Bible Hub, 2018).

According to the bible, the prophetic writing about Nebuchadnezzar is a case of divine intervention to prematurely end his misrule. Like his friend and mentor, Nelson Mandela and Moses Kotane, Kathrada was time-conscious (Venter, 2017). In this context, the possibility of South Africa's majoritarian voting population giving the ANC a further opportunity or mandate to continue as the country's governing party cannot be ruled out. The renewal of such a mandate depends on several factors. These include the ability to truly live to its ambitious programme of stability, unity towards organisational renewal, commitment to clean governance, and the implementation of a policy to find lasting solutions to the triple challenges of unemployment, poverty, and inequality (Shai & Ogunnubi, 2018; ANC Eastern Cape, 2017).

However, the existing political and socio-economic conditions at both the national and international level are not favourable to the ANC as a governing party and sustainability thereof. For example, there is a lot of pressure from within South Africa for the government to take practical measures to substantively address the economic apartheid. Consequently, the ANC government is exploring workable mechanisms to fast-track land reform programmes (Raphala, 2013). This radical approach, in the form of proposed land expropriation without compensation, seems to be currently favoured by a large segment of the black population. If this route is finally taken, it will be advantageous and disadvantageous for the ANC. On one hand, it will make the ANC popular among the majority of the voting population, at least in the short run. On the other hand, drawing lessons from the case of Zimbabwe, the radical land reform programme in South Africa might attract international reprisals in solidarity with the whites who currently own much of the land (Raphala & Shai, 2016). These reprisals will weaken South Africa's economy, which will in turn hamper the government's ability to roll out service delivery policies; a sad situation which is likely to also dampen the popularity of the party among the voters.

As hinted above, the two major highlights of Kathrada's assertions, made before millions of people mourning the death of Nelson Mandela, resonate with the popular internal description of the ANC as "the broad church". Kathrada's assertions acknowledge the diversity of South Africa as a country while the figurative description of the ANC as a broad church speaks to the diversity of its membership. The latter denotes that the ANC belongs to nationalists and pan-Africanists, whites and blacks, capitalists and socialists, just to mention a few. We argue that the figurative description of the ANC as a broad church was not well-thought out. This is because in a real church, uniform religion becomes a rallying point for the members. But in the ANC, the opening up of membership to every person is in tandem with the spirit and letter of democracy. This unchecked diversity of the membership of the ANC is the very source of the ideological and policy disagreements within the party. The latter hamstrung the historic mission of the ANC as a liberation movement-cum-ruling political party. The foregoing must be understood bearing in mind that regardless of the current diversity of its membership, the ANC has a historic obligation to promote and defend the interests of blacks and, therefore, its policy orientation ought to be pro-black.

Interweaving the ANC's political theology and morality with South Africa's internal and international relations

In 2011, the ANC-led government delayed and refused to grant a visa to the Dalai Lama, the Tibetan spiritual leader, due to the alleged diplomatic pressure from China. This decision precipitated the lashing of the ANC by Archbishop Tutu whose 80th birthday celebration the Dalai Lama was billed to honour (Thipanyane, 2011). Tutu, according to Thipanyane (2011) said the ANC-led government was "worse than the apartheid government". In principle, the government's decision to delay and/or refuse the issuing of a visa to the Dalai Lama is unjust nor did it project the ANC as a party with an entrenched theological and moral tradition. In fact, what this decision showed is that to the ANC, the country's economic interest trumps its founding African value system, which is anchored on humanity, solidary, cooperation and interdependence, among others (Mazama, 2003).

My reading of South Africa's current political landscape is that Christian virtues (ethics) have no safe space in the politics of the ANC. There is no compelling evidence that shows that such ethics play a role in strengthening the ANC as a political party (Shai, Ndaguba & Nyawasha, 2018). Instead, several cases of grand corruption and state-sponsored massacres in Marikana and elsewhere have dampened the image and integrity of the ANC and its government (Nyawasha & Mokhahlane, 2017). These societal ills have served to widen the gap between the ANC and the electorate; an unfortunate situation which has led to electoral losses for the former (ANC) (Mokgosi, Shai & Ogunnubi, 2017). While this chapter concedes that not all religious virtues are moral or ethical and not all ethical/ moral virtues are religious, it argues that political theology and morality are not exclusively distinctive and in fact, complement each other.

Conclusion

The Afrocentric study of this chapter has revealed that there are more changes than continuities in terms of the political theology and morality of the ANC. While the pre-1994 theological political rhetoric has been retained in certain instances in the new democratic dispensation, it has produced conflicting outcomes for varying generations. It is safe to conclude that the ANC identifies with the church and its doctrines when it is convenient. Thus, ANC leaders have the propensity to present themselves as presiding over Jesus Christ's kingdom until he will return to earth to assume the country/society's leadership. Besides the use of the above to attract Christian members and voters who constitute the majority of the South African population, the foregoing analysis also gives a non-Christian impression that current political and societal developments are beyond the control of Jesus Christ. But Jesus Christ is not 'dead' according to the dominant doctrine of

Christianity. In the final analysis, it was found that, in recent times, the political theology and morality of the ANC has been questioned internally and externally. This is due to the plethora of scandals that have plagued some of its prominent leaders and the party's perceived under-performance in government. As such, it is pertinent and timely to put the ANC's political theology and morality under scrutiny. To this end, this chapter sets the pace for future enquiry on this subject.

References

African National Congress Eastern Cape. 2017. Organisational renewal and design document delivered by the NEC Subcommittee on Organisational Development. http://anceasterncape.org.za/statement-on-organisational-renewal-and-design-document-delivered-by-the-chairperson-of-nec-subcommittee-on-organisational-development/ (2 July 2017).

African Christian Democratic Party (ACDP). 2019. Your ACDP: Who we are. https://www.acdp.org.za/ (7 May 2019).

Asante, M.K. 1990. Kemet, Afrocentricity and Knowledge. Trenton: Africa World Press.

Asante, M.K. 2003. Afrocentricity: The Theory of Social Change. Chicago: African American Images.

Beyers, J. 2015. Religion as political instrument: The case of Japan and South Africa. Journal for the Study of Religion, 28(1): 142-164.

Bible Gateway. 2018. Matthew 22:36-40 (King James Version). https://www.biblegateway.com/passage/?search=Matthew+22%3A36-40&version=KJV (Accessed 15 October 2018).

Bible Hub. 2018. Daniel 5:26. https://biblehub.com/parallel/daniel/5-26.htm (Accessed 17 October 2018).

Bujra, J.M. 2019. The dynamics of political action: A new look at factionalism. https://anthrosource.onlinelibrary.wiley.com/doi/pdf/10.1525/aa.1973.75.1.02a00080 (Accessed 7 May 2019).

Chetty, K. 2018. Ahmed Kathrada: A Biography. http://scnc.ukzn.ac.za/doc/B/Ks/kathrada/kathy.html (Accessed 17 October 2018).

Crafford, D. 1993. The church in Africa and the struggle for an African identity. Skrif en Kerk, 14 (2): 163-175.

Du Plessis, P.J. 2014. Perceptions of Roman empire. Fundamina, 20 (1): 216-226.

Farisani, E.B. 2014. Interpreting the bible in the context of apartheid and beyond:

An African perspective. Studia Historiae Ecclesiasticae, 40 (2): 207-225.

Koko, K. 2017. #ANC105: God is on our side, says Zuma. https://www.iol. co.za/news/politics/anc105-God-is-on-our-side-says-zuma-7347557 (Accessed 7 January 2017).

Mandela, N. 2018. A Long Walk to Freedom. https://secure.gradebookwizard. com/uploads/32637/A%20Long%20Walk%20to%20Freeom.pdf (Accessed 16 October 2018).

Manyathela, C. 2018. Zuma is harbouring hatred over how ANC treated him'. Eyewitness News. https://ewn.co.za/2018/09/10/zuma-is-harbouring-hatred-over-how-the-anc-treated-him (Accessed 10 September 2018).

Maserumule, M.H. 2011. Good governance in the New Partnership for Africa's Development (NEPAD): A public administration perspective. Unpublished PhD Thesis. Pretoria: University of South Africa.

Maserumule, M.H. 2015. Engaged scholarship and liberatory science: A professoriate, Mount Grace, and SAAPAM in the Decoloniality Mix. *Journal of Public Administration,* 50 (2): 200-222.

Mazama, A. (ed.) 2003. The Afrocentric Paradigm. Trenton: Africa World Press.

Modjadji, N. 2018. Disruptions at ANC meetings as NEC explains Zuma recall. *Sowetan Live.* https://www.sowetanlive.co.za/news/south-africa/2018-02-20-disruptions-at--anc-meetings--as-nec-explains-zuma-recall/ (Accessed 20 February 2018).

Modupe, D.S. 2003. The Afrocentric philosophical perspective: Narrative outline. In: Mazama, A. (ed.) The Afrocentric Paradigm. Trenton: Africa World Press.

Mokgosi, K., Shai, K. & Ogunnubi, O. 2017. Local government coalition in Gauteng Province of South Africa: Challenges and opportunities. Ubuntu: Journal of Conflict and Social Transformation, 6 (1): 37-57.

Molapo, R.R. 2005. Aspects of the South African youth experiences in exile, 1960-1994. Unpublished PhD thesis. Bellville: University of Western Cape.

Morgenthau, H.J. 1948. Politics Among Nations: The Struggle for Power and Peace. New York: Alfred A. Knopf.

Mzala, M. (undated). Gatsha Buthelezi: Chief with a Double Agenda. London: Zed Books.

Naidu, M. 2008. Creating an African tourist experience at the cradle of humankind World Heritage Site. Historia, 53 (2): 182-207.

Ndlovu-Gatsheni, S. J. 2018. Epistemic Freedom in Africa. London: Taylor & Francis.

Nyawasha, T. S. 2018. Post- Liberation Politics, Political Mantra and the Project of Renewal: The ANC in South Africa and ZANU-PF in Zimbabwe. (forthcoming).

Nyawasha, T.S. & Mokhahlane, P.M. 2017. The paradox of civil policing in contemporary South Africa. Insight on Africa, 9 (2): 109-125.

Pityana, N.B. 2018. The truth and reconciliation commission in South Africa: Perspectives and prospects. Journal of Global Ethics, 14 (2): 194-207.

Pretoria East Rekord. 2018. Veteran public servants receive lifetime achievement awards. https://rekordeast.co.za/183703/veteran-public-servants-receive-lifetime-achievement-awards/ (Accessed 10 September 2018).

Rankhumise, P. Shai, K. & Maphunye, M. 2008. Conflict, peace-building, human security and democratization in Lesotho. Africa Peace and Conflict Journal, 1 (1): 114-122.

Raphala, M.G. 2013. Revisiting South Africa's foreign policy towards Zimbabwe, 1999-2013. Unpublished BA Hons Dissertation. Sovenga: University of Limpopo.

Raphala, M.G. & Shai K.B. 2016. Re-evaluating the EU's external human rights and democritisation policy: a critical analysis on Zimbabwe. Governance in the 21st Century Organisations, the Proceedings of the 1st International Annual Conference on Public Administration and Development Alternatives (IPADA), The Park (Mokopane), South Africa, 06-08 July 2016.

Republic of South Africa. 1996. The Constitution, Act 108 of 1996. Pretoria: Government Printers.

Saunders, C. 2012. The ANC's 100 years: Some recent work on its history in historiographical context. Historia, 57 (2): 429-447.

Seale, W. 2017. Thabo Mbeki and the sins of incumbency. https://www.voices360.com/thabo-mbeki-and-the-sins-of-incumbency/ (Accessed 28 November 2017).

Shai, K.B. & Mothibi, K.A. 2015. Describing pre-2009 xenophobic violence in South Africa: A human right perspective. In: Sebola, M. P., Tsheola, J. P. & Mafunisa, M.J. (eds). African Governance: Society, Human Migration, State, Xenophobia and Business Contestations. Conference Proceedings. 4rd SAAPAM Limpopo Chapter Annual Conference, 28-30 October 2015.

Shai, K.B, Molapo R.R. & Sodi T. 2017. The United States of America's post-1990 foreign policy towards West Africa: The case study of Ghana. Journal for Contemporary History, 42 (1): 154-173.

Shai, K.B, Nyawasha T. S. & Ndaguba E.A. 2018. [De] constructing South Africa's Jacob Zuma led ANC: An Afrocentric perspective. Journal of Public Affairs. 2018; e1842. https://doi.org/10.1002/pa.1842

Shai, K.B. & Ogunnubi, O. 2018. [South] Africa's health system and human rights: A critical African perspective. Journal of Economics and Behavioral Studies, 10(1): 69–77.

Thipanyane, T. 2011. South Africa's foreign policy under the Zuma government: A human rights-based policy or a pragmatic approach based on political and economic considerations? AISA Policy brief, No 61 (December 2011): 1-8.

Van Wyk, T. 2015. Political theology as critical theology, HTS Teologiese Studies/ Theological Studies, 71(3): http:// dx.doi.org/10.4102/hts. v71i3.3026.

Venter, S. 2017. Conversations with a Gentle Soul. Johannesburg: Picador Africa.

West, G. 2019. Thabo Mbeki's Bible: The role of religion in the South African public realm after liberation. https://www.sbl-site.org/publications/article. aspx?ArticleId=770 (6 May 2019).

Chapter Eight

The coming of the end of the African National Congress: A reality or pipe dream?

Makhura Rapanyane

Introduction

In this chapter, the author has used Afrocentricity as a contextual lens and theoretical framework to analyse and prophesy the downfall of the ANC, happening in an environment of political multi-polarity. In essence, the principal direction derived from this chapter depicts a picture that shows how the ANC is slowly but surely going down. The fall of the ANC in this chapter is attributed to both the Zuma and Ramaphosa administrations. An effort will be made to trace policy implementation economic failures of the ANC led government in order to try to show how the ANC will not survive the challenges it is currently facing. The relevant literature was revisited in order to try to shape the current narrative around the central objective of this chapter and also show that the ANC polices which were promised in the past were unsuccessful and did not make any significant change in South Africa. The fundamental pillars of this chapter narrowed are to: analyse the costs of the Zuma administration and whether his passage of power to Ramaphosa played a significant role; highlight a continued arrogant and uncontrollable, like monster corrupt activities that continue to prevail under the administration of Ramaphosa and revisit a critical analysis of the myths and realities shaping Ramaphosa's current grasp of power. Of significance is a dissection of the rise of the key hegemonic detractors that challenged and continue to challenge the ANC's dominant status in the politics of South Africa. These detractors are analysed in this chapter as the sole reasons to drive the downfall of the ANC in the coming decade. This is not withstanding the arrogance displayed by the ANC led government, especially when such instances are slowly but surely eating from their power grip.

Research methodology

This study assumes a qualitative research approach in the form of document review and/ document analysis (Mkabela, 2005; Owusu-Ansah & Mji, 2013; Shai, 2017: 65). This research approach is one in which documents are analysed by the researcher to proffer meaning and voice on all sides of a given topic (Bowen, 2009. Equally important was the collected data which was analysed using Thematic Content Analysis (TCA) of Anderson (2017).

Theoretical contribution: Afrocentricity

In the spirit of devoting the conduct of this study as either bad or good, depending heavily on the social context (Maserumule, 2011), the author has decided to situate this research within the Afrocentric theory (read as Afrocentricity) as better explained by Asante (2003). This theory was adopted in this research as a theoretical and contextual lens because of its cognitive and functional capacity (Shai, 2019). The author has revisited the current literature on the subject of this matter and discovered that most of the studies which have been conducted suffers from the scarcity of Afrocentric perspectives (Mazama, 2003; Rapanyane & Ngoepe, 2019). The ongoing ontology in simple terms means that most of the analysis about the ANC are done without a clear Afrocentric theoretical background as the disciplines of political science and international politics have been a western construct for long till now (Ndlovu-Gatsheni, 2018). It is for the reason of this nature that, an Afrocentric attempt employed in this chapter serve as a way to curb the marginalization of African concepts, philosophies, theories, by Africans for Africans, like Afrocentricity (Maserumule, 2015). The fundamental principle of Afrocentricity and also the central objective is to ensure that every knowledge of reality about the phenomenon of Africa should be found in studies conducted by Africans who have applied African value systems, tools and standards (Asante, 1990). In this research, the author has adopted the instructive model to all readers to note that the theory's analytical categories as better articulated by Modupe (2003) have been adopted and invoked in this study as they shape all Afrocentric studies. These are Grounding which remains a procedure of learning, highly centered on African people, their culture, history and continent. The second is orientation which preaches "having and pursuing intellectual interest in the African and the formation of a psychological identity direction, based upon that interest, in the direction toward Africa" (Shai, 2019). Third and last is perspective which designates self-awareness of seeing and exerting influence on the world in a way that give significance to the interests of Africans and "which is suggestive of the quality, kind and amount of the above-mentioned two elements" (Shai, 2019).

Any revolutionary divergence from the above prescribed analytical elements in the adoption of Afrocentricity is often referred to as the "transversal error" (Shai, 2017). The foregoing illustration does not really mean that alternative theories are dismantled in understanding the subject of this nature. They are embraced as they also assist us in understanding political issues in Africa and the South African context (Rapanyane, 2018). The fundamental point propagated in this research is that, Afrocentricity should be seen as the only relevant way to analyze African political issues (Rapanyane & Ngoepe, 2019). Given the fact that theories and concepts like systems can borrow from each other for the fundamental idea of self-development, it will then be perceivable and very much fair to afford

Afrocentricity an equal chance to co-exist with its western counterparts in order to generate a new alternative and fresh naked truths to conventional knowledge (Asante, 2003).

Literature review: Failed economic policy implementation, 1994-2017

RDP and GEAR

RDP was a policy of the ANC that was planned before the general elections of 1994 as a very determined national policy project which was poised to be all-inclusive (Brits, 2017: 507). The "RDP base document", an initiative of the ANC led tripartite Alliance which became a comprehensive charter which reiterated some of the fundamental pillars outlined in the freedom charter. At the beginning, the implementation of the RDP as a policy framework for South Africa was afforded only 2.5 billion from the national budget and this money was never enough to curb the log-jam in the service provisions and realise equal infrastructure to the those who were underprivileged and marginalised by the Apartheid regime (Luiz, 2007). Amongst the reasons why the RDP failed is due to its lack of implementation and coordination required skills in the ranks of the ANC, trustworthiness of the then ANC civil servants which was time to time questioned and also various intra-organisation pitfalls. Another factor was the scarcity of the relevant resources required for the implementation of this policy (Luiz, 2007; Wallis 1995). These sentiments meant that the ANC was unable to master the RDP policy and make it a successful socio-economic policy. It was after the country's currency depreciation and volatility that Trevor Manuel (Former Minister of Finance) on the 14th of June 1996 made an announcement to replace RDP with the Growth, Employment and Redistribution (GEAR) strategy as the new policy programme in parliament (Abedian & Ajam, 2009: 82). After this announcement, the ANC government made it clear that RDP was built on the elements of RDP and sought to achieve some of the RDP objectives (Jeffery, 2010: 245).

The proposed GEAR was implemented as a policy programme that wanted to rebuild and reshape the economy of South Africa in conjunction with policy initiatives set out in the RDP (Jeffery, 2010: 245). In essence, the policy of GEAR was actually premised upon the fundamental element of free market stratagem with the idea of re-diverting attention to economic growth (Brits, 2014: 507). Although it became a success in other areas, this policy failed dismally in other areas. The gains which were recorded in the budget were accompanied by catastrophic social costs. So inequality and poverty levels were increased extremely in the years before it became a policy framework (Habib, 2013: 81). In essence, the growth rate that was recorded during GEAR never surpassed 5% of which was in contradictory to what was promised prior its implementation of growing the economy with 6%. GEAR brought close to 30% unemployment rate with it (Gevisser, 2009: 252). In the year 2000, the GDP recorded a lessened Foreign Direct Investment (FDI) of which was accompanied by a decrease in the employment in the non-agricultural activities of 3.3% (Mosala, et al., 2017).

Due to this diminishing employment and savage austerity, the principal after effect of this was a continual inequality. Emerging from the above sentiments, it becomes quite clear that South Africans really did not enjoy the benefits of the promised GEAR and as a result, was actually replaced by the Accelerated and Shared Growth Initiative- South Africa (ASGISA) in 2006 (Mosala, et al., 2017).

ASGISA and NGP

ASGISA was a policy blueprint that was announced by Phumzile Mlambo-Ngcuka (Former South African Deputy President) in the year 2005 and was only launched a year later in 2006. The main idea behind the execution of ASGISA as a replacement of GEAR was to curb the already increased unemployment rate in the country as well as poverty rate by the year 2014 (Anon, 2006). This was in line with the already set Millennium Development Goals (MDGs). Another objective of ASGISA was to bring an improvement to the environments of economic performance capacity and job creation in South Africa. Since it was afforded a little time of execution, it really became an impossible task to measure its failures and successes or otherwise. Though, honestly, it recorded progress in the area of infrastructure especially in the public sector spending with an increment to 9.6% from 4.6% for the period of 4 years between 2006 to 2010 (Mbola, 2009). Unemployment and poverty rates remained the same and, in some instance, increased after it was implemented. ASGISA was replaced with New Growth Path (NGP) during the last days of then President Thabo Mbeki in highest office in the land (Mosala, et al., 2017).

As a policy blueprint that replaced ASGISA, NGP was announced by then President Jacob Zuma in 2010 during his State of the Nation Address (SONA). As policy that built upon the failures of NGP, its principal objectives were to do away with the country's huge unemployment rate, inequalities and poverty rates (Morris, 2013). The policy as deliberated was announced with the intention of curing unemployment rate and reducing it with 10% by at least creating 5 million jobs by 2020 by using infrastructural programmes (Gumede, 2012). However, the execution of this policy was also afforded a short period of time and as such, its effectiveness and/ successes cannot simply be measured especially in consideration of the fact that it takes time to execute a country's national economic policy (Gumede, 2012). Therefore, the National Development Plan (NDP) was introduced and planned on top of the NGP objectives to be only implemented from 2012 (Mosala, et al., 2017).

NDP and RET

NDP became the most favoured, in fact, the biggest macroeconomic policy of the ANC led government. The NDP preached economic growth as a way that will reduce the trio economic problems of poverty, unemployment and inequality. In essence, this policy blueprint was a stretched long vision of up to the year 2030 (NPC, 2012). Thus, by 2013, NDP sought to achieve the following objectives: unite all South Africans of all classes and races towards a common means to reduce inequality and poverty rates. Secondly, motivate all citizens of South Africa in being active in strengthening their own developmental democracy and ensuring that their government practices accountability. Third, increase economic development, promote exports and ensure that the South African economy is highly labour intensive. NDP also sought to redirect focus towards the principal capabilities of the country and the people. These are infrastructure, skills, social security, partnerships with international partners and within South Africa as well as strengthening the state institutions. To add, it also sought to build a developmental and capable state (NDP, 2019). Equally important was to enhance a strong societal leadership that had the ambition of solving the societal problems. In line with the objectives of the NDP, by the year 2030, South Africa had to have curbed poverty expressed by households with incomes below R419 monthly per person. And also a huge cutback in existing inequalities recorded in the Gini Coefficient to 0.6 from 0.69 (NDP, 2019).

Even if this NDP was envisioned up to the year 2030, Zuma still announced Radical Economic Transformation (RET) as a policy framework in his 2017 Jan 8 ANC speech, by arguing that South Africa needed RET. Initially, RET is a policy that intended to focus on land redistribution, inclusive economic development and also terminating white monopoly capital practises (Mostert, 2015). Osthuizen (2016) believes that RET is a result of the failed efforts to safeguard the socio-economic rights that have been violated for the past three decades for millions of South Africans. Alternatively, Mutize and Gooseland (2017) have reasoned that the pillars of RET have been outlined well by Zuma who had argued that RET in essence is about doing away with white monopoly capital when he also put a blame on this tendency which has marginalised South African black majority from the mainstream economy in the previous decades of the ANC government. Both Mutize and Gooseland (2017) argue that RET should not be considered a new concept as it has been previously used by ANC government to shift attention away from the problems facing South Africa's economy. Principal pillars of the RET included:

> Returning land to our people and supporting land reform, increasing black ownership and control in the economy, Activating small businesses and co-operatives, Raising the level of investment, Strengthening social justice and conditions for the poor and working class, Improving the employment impact of infrastructure projects, Reducing inequality and poverty, Dismantling monopoly practices and structures, Improving integration into the African economy, Stimulating inclusive growth (ANC 2017).

From Zuma to Ramaphosa: No change, but worst expectations?

In trying to shape the research for this chapter, the author has revisited the works of a number of scholars who have written about the aspects which have downgraded the hegemonic status of the ANC in South Africa. Writers such as Bisseker (2018), Cilliers (2018), Adonis (2019), Steyn (2018), Menon & Mkentane (2019), Head

(2019), Ramorei (2019), Muller (2019) and Malada (2018). Bisseker (2018) has written an online article titled "R1-trillion: the cost of the Zuma years" in which he has analysed the costs of the Zuma administration on the South African economy. Bisseker argues that the economy of South Africa could have created at least 2.5 million jobs and R1 trillion extra money had it kept the pace with other economies in the region. He further extends that "SA's economic stagnation between 2010 and 2017 cost the country in terms of the growth, taxes and jobs forgone" and highlights that the Zuma presidential years should be referred to as the lost years as "real GDP would have been 15.4% (R481bn) higher by the end of 2017". Cilliers (2018) on the other side indicates that by 2018, South Africa was R1 trillion poorer because of the presidential years of Zuma. Cilliers interjects that the above sentiments expressed by Bisseker were as a result of the poor economic performance and loss of efficiency in tax revenue collection. He argues that the BER Economist Harry Kemp's findings in the "Ten Years After the Lehman collapse: SA's Post-Crisis Performance in Perspective" report which discovered the same findings presented by Bisseker. Adonis (2019) in "how Zuma's illegal R1 trillion nuclear deal led to Eskom Crisis" says that both the Earthlife Africa and the Southern African Faith Communities' Environmental Institute (SAFCEI) took the government of South Africa to court over the controversial nuclear deal in order for the government to withdraw their nuclear plans as both organisations blamed the obsession of Zuma with the Russian deal on the intensification of the country's energy crisis at Eskom. Adonis had shown that the Zuma administration has brought nothing but an attempt to impose a nuclear deal which had the capacity to require the country's entire annual budget which was needed for public services such as education and health care.

Steyn (2018) in his online article "budget 2018 is Zuma's costly legacy" has observed that the budget of 2018 had depicted signs of damage done by Zuma's years in power by demolishing the institutions of the State and also adding more governmental bill of 57 billion for higher education which manifested in the governmental need to impose decisions such as the hiking Value Added Tax (VAT). In his article, Steyn has deliberated that the budget was "legacy of Jacob Zuma's disastrous management of the economy of South Africa". In essence, Steyn champions the view that "Much of the low growth is a direct result of the past political environment" which was a direct result of low tax morality. Even after Zuma has stepped down from Power, South Africa still faces persisting triple socio-economic challenges, unemployment, inequality and poverty. Menon & Mkentane (2019) have shown in the online article titled "Cyril Ramaphosa faces surging unemployment problem" that Ramaphosa is still to work on the unemployment rate which continues to grow and even nears 30% mark. In their analysis, they have shown that Ramaphosa's top list of priorities should be the issues such as strengthening the country's economy on a robust growth rate and also curbing the unemployment rate. In their (Menon & Mkentane, 2019) analysis, they illustrate that unemployment rate has jumped to 29%, higher than ever expected, and this incident was last seen in the year 2003. They also argue that this unemployment rate was a direct result of the years of economic mismanagement and that Ramaphosa's direct promise of the 2 Million jobs over 10 years when the country has this highest number of unemployment rate standing at 6.7 million people without jobs worldwide is an admission of a defeat. The foregoing sentiments are supported by Head (2019). Head (2019) attests that based on Ramaphosa "the country is on course for a dramatic loss of jobs in the coming years" and this is because of the four major challenges of: Firstly, low economic growth due to failed and failing State Owned Enterprises (SOEs) with a rich history of corruption. Secondly, Globalisation in which South African traders are not capaciated to compete with foreign markets. Third, Climate change, in which extreme weather events of droughts are slowly destroying the country's agricultural industry. Fourth and last, Technology, which will result in the tech-knowledge increment, consequentially leading to the more jobs autmated, decreaing the need for human input. Ramorei (2019) projects that the fundamental problem experienced by South Africa is the problem of monopolies which have predominated the country's economy and continue to prevent the coming in of new players and even in the banking sectors such as Absa, FNB, Nedbank and Standard bank and that Ramaphosa himself has admitted that the economy of South Africa has not changed its apartheid/ colonial structure since the year 1994. Even though this is the case, Muller (2019) contends that South Africa's public finances is in trouble due to these four reasons. First, low economic growth, below forecast tax revenue collection, high levels of debts and impoverished perfomance of SOEs which continuasly necessitate state bailouts. Muller does not shy away from indicating that:

> The state of SA's public finances is the outcome of different dynamics in three overlapping periods. The first was the period after the 2008 global financial crisis. The second was the period under Jacob Zuma's presidency. And the third has been the period since Cyril Ramaphosa took over (2019).

Muller further advises that "In the face of the crisis, the only way to proceed is to secure a social compact that recognises the need for sacrifices. Ramaphosa is uniquely equipped to secure this. But he is moving too slowly". However, Madala (2018) argues that the concept of the New Dawn as proposed by Ramaphosa "is figuratively and literally short-sighted. It lacks long-term perspective. It is already losing steam and will not last". Madala's main points are that, South Africans should be careful of political catchy statements, erratic at worst and best elusive. Madala has further articulated that "The metaphor of a new dawn may sound poetic, but dawn is, by nature, a very short time in the totality of the 24 hours that see each day come and pass". Madala also quoted Hendrik van Der Bijl who observed that ambition actually has to do with desiring fame, honour, power and excellence. He also added that, the same concept is very much virtuous and can be vicious as it attracts ignorance in its noble form; it is vainglorious and remains unselfish. In the end, Madala (2019) has advised that as Zuma's term of office was a "long winter of despair, Ramaphosa's season of hope must not lull South Africans into a culture of dependency. South Africans must wake up from the slumber of the new dawn and embrace a new age of ambition".

The ongoing fever of a corrupt state: 2018-2019

Nkanjeni (2019) is actually in line with the 10th Edition of the Global Corruption Barometer (GCB) Africa, and it is very much clear as it shows that the findings of the African Anti-Corruption Suvery conducted by the Transparency International are of the discovery that 75% of the South Africans still believe that the South African government was not concerned with the corrupt scandals in the country. As such, most of the issues as Nkanjeni (2019) depicts them, were surrounded around corrupt public institutions and officials, more especially, the police service with atleast 49% of the local South Africans beliving that all police officers are corrupt. The main problem in the police service is driven by bribery. Practically, the interlinkage of the corrupt scandals recorded in the police service is the same with the one recorded in local governments and Members of Parliament (MPs) which stood at 44%, though they denounced corruption in the Non-Governmental Organisations (NGOs). De-Vos (2019) believes that Ramaphosa is actually not in a good standing to end patrogane and corruption because he assumed the position of the presidency with support from various groups of elites who are implicated in corruption. De-Vos (2019) has qouted Von Holdt who urged that:

> The staunchly pro-Ramaphosa leadership of the Eastern Cape are implicated in the plundering and institutional decay of Nelson Mandela Bay detailed in (Crispian) Olver's 2016 book. The deputy chair of the ANC in KwaZulu-Natal, who played a leading role in mobilising support for Ramaphosa in that Zuma-supporting province, Mike Mabuyakhulu, has just been indicted in court with seven co-accused for corruption and money- laundering. Not only was Mpumalanga s support crucial to Ramaphosa s victory as noted above, DD Mabuza s position as deputy president puts him in line for the presidency in 10 years time.

Secondly, Ramaphosa did not win a majority vote, therefore, less authority in the ANC as he carefully moves well to regain authority by establishing the unification strategy for those who are implicated in corrupt scandals and those who are not. As such, Ramaphosa faces the challenge of vulnerability to populist challenges like Zuma did to Mbeki and that the alternative corrupt faction may see him as a greater threat should he try to shut down the total access to state resources for wealth accumulation by aspirant elites and this will lead to backlash. The same pessimistic sentiments expressed by De-Vos (2019) are those expressed by Von-Holdt (2019) who has observed that "any South Africans do not think that Ramaphosa will be forced to reverse course because their understanding of corruption in South Africa is far too simplistic".

Myths and realities surrounding ANC's current weaknesses

Not so long ago during Ramaphosa's Maiden SONA were South Africans grappled with his new concept of the 'New dawn' which left South Africans with a positive mind and positive restart after a long political battle with the corrupt scandalous Zuma regime. At his inauguration, many were positive and came forward to outline their expectations of the incumbent (Ngcobo, 2019). For Tokyo Sexwale, Ramaphosa's new concept of the 'New Dawn' was an inspiring one quoted as indicating that: *"The president has proclaimed that we are in the middle of a dawn. The dawn is not sunrise, it's just the beginning of the light. We must move with the dawn so that we can have the sun shining over South Africa, in all the different corners of the country where people who cannot be here today are,"* Sexwale added (Maya-Rose, 2019).

To the best analysis of this chapter: 'New Dawn', Ramaphosa's political famous concept was never given too much media attention. That is why this concept has remained a mystery and/ conundrum since its inception. Where spotted, this concept has been interpreted differently by different scholars, political reporters and people in general. What is most popular about this concept is that it is pillared by the four objectives as better articulated by Ramaphosa (Lediga, 2018). These are clean governance and intensified anti-corrupt drive, rebuilding South Africa's broken economy, pay special attention to education and training and also *thuma mina* as led by his famous quote of "Ask not what your country can do for you, but what you can do for your country" (Lediga, 2018). To add, Hugh Masekela's profound song 'send me'. He then termed this as the 'New Dawn' (Sidiropoulos, 2018). Now what needs to be questioned here is: Is the New Dawn campaign still in action? Perhaps it was going to be better if Ramaphosa spoke precisely of how the 'New Dawn' is to unfold and what promises entailed the 'New Dawn' in the past 16 months as the incumbent and also during his latest SONA in June 2019.

'Ramaphoria' is what has entered the vocabulary of South Africans after South Africa's positive political transformations of 2018. Thus, after his election as the President of South Africa replacing Zuma after his forced resignation, a wave of optimism in the sense of brand new modalities from ethics to policy implementation crossed South Africa (Hogg, 2018). But it is hard to admit that since Zuma's resignation in 2018, things have changed in the internal dynamics of the ANC in the sense that the ANC had become soft and compromising to see reality. This is especially after the motion on land expropriation without compensation was passed as championed by Economic Freedom Fighters (EFF), the ANC was coerced and politically cornered to end up voting on amendment with EFF (Van-Zyl, 2018). Not only this was a political surprise to South Africans but also a new economic stagnation that hit South Africa's socio-economic and political landscapes hard on the eve of June 2018 when Statistics South Africa (StatsSA) reported that South Africa's economy declined by 2.2% which was the greatest contraction quarter to quarter since Zuma's inauguration in 2009 leading to a question of whether Ramaphosa is really the darling of the people and international investors (Mathe, 2019).

It is clear that, really something was wrong with the ANC. After the general elections on May 2019, there were speculations all over the world as to who is to serve in the Ramaphoria cabinet to make a fertile ground for international investment (with job opportunities and economic growth in mind). But it was clear to Ramaphosa that South Africa needed brand new faces in cabinet and experiential candidates together in the name of Gender balance for equity in the new cabinet to take South Africa forward (Hunter, 2019). With this being said it is argumentative that South Africa's new 2019 cabinet composed of ANC comrades and politicians whom, if not all were once accused of corruption like David Mabuza (Deputy President) (Onishi & De-Greef, 2019) and implicated in State Capture inquiries and of which some were expected to be reprimanded as-per the advises of the Public Protector Busisiwe Mkhwebane, right from the top branches of his government as promised, jeopardizing his reform agenda (Quintal & Mailovich, 2019). After being in office for two months now, South Africans have noted significant changes in the Ramaphosa takeover of the ANC power helms, as serious transformations in the ANC took place such as the introductory of new faces in the cabinet and that cabinet portfolios trimmed to 28 from 36 of which he was applauded for (Nicolson, 2019). Not only was he applauded for appointments and cabinet trimming but for also ensuring that he includes competence, continuity, experience and also generational mix together with gender balance (African-News-Agency, 2019).

But after the elections, South Africans waited for the 20th June 2019 when Ramaphosa was expected to stand in front of the nation and inform them on his plans to take the country a way forward in the sense of tabling plans of actions on how to reverse the last 9 years of the Zuma administration, and shed thousands of jobs for young people, and also expropriate land without compensation as promised (Writer, 2019). What is important is that the saint promises made by ANC government during the May 2019 elections could not in anyhow be fulfilled by one man. Thus, it should be that the people he appointed to the cabinet should all have a hand in the accomplishment of all those promises as required by the proportional representation model that empowers political parties over public representatives. Apart from this, Ramaphosa's latest SONA shows that South Africans must dream of a better future with trains, new cities, 2 million job opportunities for the next decade (Gerber, 2019), and if so, what about the promised "land expropriation without compensation"?

The sentiment: Ramaphosa's SONA was a tasteless statement of intention without anything tangible to peg it on could be truthful to some extent (Marrian, 2019). The seven priorities as set out by Ramaphosa outlines education, skills and health, economic transformation and job creation, consolidating the social wage through reliable and quality basic services, social cohesion and safe communities, spatial integration, human settlements and local government, a better Africa and World and a capable, ethical and developmental state are some of the significant objectives needed by South Africa for a better future (Marrian, 2019). In extension, Ramaphosa promised that violent crimes will be reduced and schools will have better education outcomes and no South African citizen will go hungry. Of importance is his dreams which extends to bullet trains and construction of a new city (Payne, 2019).

What is most surprising is that, in a country that records 9 million youth unemployment and/ +50% youth unemployment rate, the president promises only 2 million jobs for the next 10 years (Madisa, 2019). This has been ushered without a clear quantifiable objective outlining how in the short to medium term, certain issues will be tackled. What is also important is that, it is a matter of fact that the NDP promises at least 11 million jobs by 2030 (NDP Vision 2030) of which Ramaphoria-era does not see it possible and a reality, but promises only two million jobs in the next coming decade. What is also spotted is that Ramaphosa said that "those who dreamt of a better life gave him hope" (Du-Plessis, 2019). Ramaphosa further outlined that he "wanted to see bullet trains in South Africa, and the creation of new cities, as had been done with great success in countries like China" (Du-Plessis, 2019).

In context, the president alludes that "All this is with the doers who are able to get things done, not just the people who sit by the side-lines and scream and shout" he added. After saying all these statements, few hours passed after he finished with SONA address and another political surprise hit South Africa's political landscape when Maggie Sotyu who is the deputy minister of environment, fisheries and forestry took to media a picture of Ramaphosa "with a thought bubble containing a bullet train, and the caption, in capital letters: "HE'S DREAMING!!"(Du-Plessis, 2019). Even though Sotyu commented by saying that South Africans who poked the president were wasting time and made reference of Martin Luther King's famous quote of a "I have a dream" speech of 1963, it is still to be questioned whether the President's dream is enough for the people of South Africa. To support Ramaphosa's dreams, Magashule who is the Secretary general of the ANC alluded that "What the president has said is not his dream, it's the people's dream, the nation's dream which is going to be realised" (Van-Diemen, 2019). What is troublesome is whether the tabling of this dream by the president and his ANC comrades is enough for South African youth and the significant issue of land expropriation without compensation which if executed could empower majority of the black poor South Africans and capacitate them with farming skills in order for them to make a better life. To add, South Africans are still waiting for the ANC government to correct the mistakes of the 9 lost years of the Zuma-era not just with dreams but a plan of action (Writer, 2019). South Africa's youth is facing a socio-economic problem which is also distressing in the sense that they are sitting at home doing nothing on a daily basis and in the next decade, they are still likely to be doing nothing, as out of 9 million jobs needed, only 2 million will be delivered, if possible, together with a continuous delay on the process of land reform.

Hegemonic dominance detractors: towards a total failure and dismantling of the ANC

29% unemployment rate

South Africans woke up to an increased unemployment rate which moved from 27.6% to 29% on the 30th of July 2019. This number has placed a number of people who are unemployed at 6.7 million in line with StatsSA's findings (Smit, 2019). In his SONA on the 20 June 2019, Ramaphosa admitted that this problem of youth unemployment has become "a national crisis that demands urgent, innovative and coordinated solutions where all of us should see it as a requirement to work together" (The-Presidency, 2019). Drawing from his statement, the author of this chapter argues that the unemployment rate that continues to haunt the unemployed youth of South Africa will be the same to convince themselves that the ANC is no longer effective in terms of delivering their promises.

The growth of EFF: An exchange with the ANC's downfall

During the last elections, the EFF experienced a dramatic growth, moving from 6.35% to now 10.79% with 44 MPs in the parliament (Grobler, 2019). Du-Toit (2019) has quoted Scholtz who indicated that "it is clear from the numbers that the ANC's losses represent gains by Julius Malema's EFF". The above indicated statement alludes that the growing of the EFF has affected and continues to affect the ANC immensely, as when the alternative left, EFF continues to record growth, the ANC on the other side, continues to record a decline in terms of MPs. So, since it has become clear that South Africans have given the ANC one last chance again, after promising to deliver the land to the poor of the poorest, and now it is again playing a delaying tactics. This will make South Africans to have to opt for the EFF in the upcoming elections.

2 million jobs, instead of 11 million jobs promised in the NDP

Out of the 11 Million Jobs indicated by the NDP vision 2030, Ramaphosa during his SONA on June 20 only promised 2 million jobs in the next 10 years of his administration of which Mavuso (2019) says it is just a pipe dream. The same pipe dream, Menon & Mkentane (2019) refers to as an admission of defeat. The admission of the defeat in this case means that Ramaphosa has finally admitted that there will be no jobs to be created to half the unemployment rate that is already at 29% in the next coming decade of his administration. Practically, this means that his administration will do nothing for the unemployed youth and that those who are in higher education institutions can just forget about being employed upon their completions.

State capture: An ongoing costly process in the midst of 29% unemployment rate

State Capture is a process that emanates from the activities of the economic powerful elites who are influencing the decision-making processes in the public sector for the principal objective of narrow and selfish goals (Shai, 2017). After realising how the ANC had been operating under so many State Capture corruption scandals in the last 3 decades, Zuma decided that he would appoint a judicial commission of inquiry into State Capture (Grace, 2018). As it stands now, the State Capture commission of Inquiry has managed to wipe out at least above R356 million, to be paid from the State coffers (Sibanda & Lekubu, 2019). In her report Appel (2018) had articulated that the State Capture was expected to run for at least two years with millions cost on the public purse and further asks: is it really worth it? Friedman (2019) has shown that by September 2019, the rental property of redefine properties and Tiso black star have both cost the commission of inquiry at least 14.8 million, making R1.2 million per month to come from the public purse. It is important to highlight that event though it remains a remedial action, it continues to cost South African tax payers millions every month.

Fallacious New Dawn

The concept of the New Dawn in essence was Ramaphosa's campaign strategy to inspire hope into South Africans of a new change and/ a new beginning for South Africans. The concept of the New Dawn is just similar to the Ramaphoria-era wave that crossed South Africa when Ramaphosa replaced Zuma as the president (Ngcobo, 2019). He was seen as a 'breath of fresh air' (Mofokeng, 2019). Ramaphosa positioned himself as the 'Messiah' who was going to bring South Africans to the land of milk and honey (Mofokeng, 2019). To amass South African support, he introduced the catchphrase of the New Dawn in which he spoke of how he planned to deal with corruption deep-rooted in the ANC. But practically, Ramaphosa's New Dawn is actually a proven fallacy with no direction or stable policy framework to turn South Africa's economy around (Mofokeng, 2019). In his book, titled, *"After Dawn: Hope after state capture"*, Mcebisi Jonas says that the so-called New dawn is quickly dying (Modise, 2019). Not only is it quickly dying, but it never really existed as it was always a myth. To support this Heller & Seepe (2019) argued that "South Africa is a nation that oscillates between hope and hopelessness" and that "This national psychosis is at the heart of the propagandist portrait of President Ramaphosa as the salve and salvation of South Africa". The financial mail (2019) argues that the end of Ramaphoria of 2018 has come and that it is now dead and that the fragility of the so called New Dawn as a replacement of Ramaphoria has shown South Africans that indeed the next phase is becoming Ramaphantasy as the number of unemployment rate inclusive of discouraged jobseekers hit 38.5% on the 1st of August 2019. Now, if this is the case, who is still sure if Ramaphosa is really capable of delivering South Africans to the land of milk and honey?

Analysis and conclusion

In this chapter, the author has discovered that in terms of policy implementation, no economic policy of the ANC has been able to solve the triple socio-economic problems of poverty, unemployment and inequality in South Africa since 1994 *(a curse passed on from Apartheid White agents)*. The implication, drawn from this statement, in essence means that Mandela, Mbeki and Motlanthe administrations have failed in their attempts to take black South Africans who were previously marginalised to the promised land of milk and honey. By the same token, South Africans were not surprised when the latest Zuma administration has instead cost the South African public purse immensely. This is because his administration has been repeatedly involved in corrupt scandals which have continued to deplete the country's public purse for selfish gains. Equally important was a critical inquiry into the possibility of the Ramaphosa administration to curb the problems highlighted above, though as we stand currently, such seems impossible as

Ramaphosa himself has admitted that South Africa is yet to experience mass losses of jobs. Practically and honestly speaking, the problem of poverty should be interlinked with unemployment because if South Africans are not employed, they will continue to swim in the poverty circles. Despite this, one fundamental alternative discovery in this chapter was that, the Ramaphosa administration is full of confusions, dreams, fallacies, fantasies and misleading promises. This continues to deepens pain into the South African unemployed youth who had hope when he ascended to the presidency in 2019, replacing Zuma. The most pertinent case point was that of the promised 2 million jobs in the coming 10 years which has been changed now to mass losses of jobs. The fundamental reasons given above which illustrate the myths and realities surrounding Ramaphosa's first few months in office shows well that he is not ready to move South Africa forward. In fact, backward, the ANC's hegemonic detractors which are discussed on a broader analysis such as the increasing unemployment rate, the rise of the alternative left, EFF, mass losses of jobs statement/ utterance, State Capture funding and the fallacious statements which are continuing to be the order of the day and the so-called New Dawn are the ones which will accompany the ANC to its grave in the coming 10 years.

References

Abedian, I. & Ajam, T. 2009. Fiscal policy beyond 2008: Prospects, risks, and opportunities. In Parson, R (ed). Zumanomics: which way to Shared Prosperity in South Africa? Challenges for a New Government. Johannesburg: Jacana Media. .

Adonis, N. 2019. How Zuma's illegal R1-trillion nuclear deal led to the ESKOM crisis. [Online] Available at: http://www.ngopulse.org/press-release/how-zuma%E2%80%99s-illegal-r1-trillion-nuclear-deal-led-eskom-crisis [Accessed 08 10 2019].

African-News-Agency, 2019. New cabinet shows focus on accelerated inclusive economic growth - Agbiz. [Online] Available at: https://www.iol.co.za/business-report/economy/new-cabinet-shows-focus-on-accelerated-inclusive-economic-growth-agbiz-24444082[Accessed 12 10 2019].

ANC, 2017. Economic transformation: ANC discussion document 2017. [Online] Available at: https://www.politicsweb.co.za/opinion/economic-transformation-ancdiscussion-document-20 [Accessed 13 10 2019].

Anderson, R. 2017. Thematic Content Analysis (TCA): Descriptive Presentation of Qualitative Data.. [Online] Available at: www.rosemarieanderson.com. [Accessed 06 10 2019].

Anonymous, 2006. What is Asgisa? Fin24archives. [Online] Available at: http://www.fin24.com/Economy/What-is-Asgisa20060707 [Accessed 08 10 2019].

Appel, M. 2018. Just how much will the state capture inquiry cost?. [Online]

Available at: https://www.enca.com/analysis/just-how-much-will-state-capture-inquiry-cost[Accessed 10 10 2019].

Asante, M.K. 1990. Kemet, Afrocentricity and Knowledge. Trenton: Africa World Press.

Asante, M.K. 2003. Afrocentricity: The Theory of Social Change. Chicago: African American Images.

Bisseker, C. 2018. R1-trillion: the cost of the Zuma years. [Online] Available at: https://www.timeslive.co.za/politics/2018-10-12-r1-trillion-the-cost-of-the-zuma-years/ [Accessed 08 10 2019].

Bowen, G. 2009. Document analysis as a qualitative research method.. Qualitative Research Journal, 9(2), pp. 27-40.

Brits, J. 2014. South Africa after apartheid, 1994–2004. In: Pretorius, F. (ed.) A History of South Africa: From the Distant Past to the Present Day. Pretoria: Protea Book House.

Cilliers, C. 2018. SA R1 trillion poorer due to the 'Zuma years', report finds. [Online] Available at: https://citizen.co.za/news/south-africa/2023252/sa-r1-trillion-poorer-due-to-the-zuma-years-report-finds/[Accessed 08 10 2019].

De-Vos, P. 2019. Why Ramaphosa is probably not in a position to end corruption and patronage. [Online] Available at: https://www.dailymaverick.co.za/article/2019-04-29-why-ramaphosa-is-probably-not-in-a-position-to-end-corruption-and-patronage/ [Accessed 09 10 2019].

Du-Plessis, 2019. Member of Ramaphosa's government mocks his dream of a future city, bullet train. [Online] Available at: https://www.dailymaverick.co.za/article/2019-06-23-member-of-ramaphosas-government-mocks-his-dream-of-a-future-city/[Accessed 10 10 2019].

Du-Toit, P. 2019. News24 Projects: ANC on 57%, DA declines and EFF grows. [Online] Available at: https://www.news24.com/elections/news/news24-projects-anc-on-57-da-declines-and-eff-grows-20190509[Accessed 12 10 2019].

Financialmail, 2019. Editorial: New dawn to dust. [Online] Available at: https://www.businesslive.co.za/fm/opinion/editorial/2019-08-01-editorial-new-dawn-to-dust/[Accessed 10 10 2019].

Friedman, D. 2019. Venue rental for Zondo Commission has cost us R14.8m so far, reveals De Lille. [Online] Available at: https://citizen.co.za/news/south-africa/state-capture/2177174/venue-rental-for-zondo-commission-has-cost-us-r14-8m-so-far-reveals-de-lille/[Accessed 10 10 2019].

Gerber, J. 2019. SONA: Dream, dream, filling up an idle hour and 20 minutes. [Online] Available at: https://www.news24.com/SouthAfrica/News/sona-dream-

dream-filling-up-an-idle-hour-and-20-minutes-20190621[Accessed 14 10 2019].

Gevisser, M. 2009. Thabo Mbeki: The Dream Deferred. Cape Town: Jonathan Ball Publishers.

Grace, J. 2018. Commission of inquiry into state capture – do we really need it and will it *happen?*. [Online] Available at: https://constitutionallyspeaking. co.za/commission-of-inquiry-into-state-capture-do-we-really-need-it-and-will-it-happen/[Accessed 10 10 2019].

Grobler, R. 2019. EFF on huge growth: 'Thank you, South Africa'. [Online] Available at: https://www.news24.com/elections/news/eff-on-huge-growth-thank-you-south-africa-20190513[Accessed 10 10 2019].

Gumede, W. 2012. Restless Nation: Making Sense of Troubled Times. Cape Town: Tafelberg.

Habib, A. 2013. South Africa's Suspended Revolution: Hopes and Prospects. Johannesburg: Wits University Press.

Head, T. 2019. Cyril Ramaphosa gives four reasons why "many more jobs will be lost" *in SA*. [Online] Available at: https://www.thesouthafrican.com/news/cyril-ramaphosa-jobs-losses-why-how-to-fix/[Accessed 07 10 2019].

Heller, K. & Seepe, S. 2019. The collapse of the New Dawn myth. [Online] Available at: https://www.iol.co.za/news/ opinion/the-collapse-of-the-new-dawn-myth-31049611 [Accessed 10 10 2019].

Hogg, A. 2018. Ramaphoria infecting SA like a happy virus – consumer confidence surges to all-time high. [Online] Available at: https://www.biznews. com/good-hope-project/2018/04/25/ramaphoria-consumer-confidence-surges [Accessed 08 10 2019].

Hunter, Q. 2019. Who's in and who's out of SA's 2019 cabinet. [Online] Available at: https://www.timeslive.co.za/politics/2019-05-30-a-listicle-of-who-is-in-and-who-is-out-of-sa-cabinet-2019/[Accessed 10 10 2019].

Jeffery, A. 2010. Chasing the Rainbow: South Africa's move from Mandela to Zuma. Johannesburg: South African Institute of Race Relations.

Lediga, S. 2018. The four pillars of Ramaphosa's New Dawn. [Online] Available at: https://www.dailymaverick.co.za/opinionista/2018-05-07-the-four-pillars-of-ramaphosas-new-dawn/[Accessed 05 10 2019].

Luiz, J. 2007. The battle for social and economic policy. Discourse Wits Business School - University of the Witwatersrand, 35(2).

Madisa, K. 2019. Ramaphosa promises two million jobs for youth in the next 10 years. [Online] Available at: https://www.sowetanlive.co.za/news/south-africa/2019-06-20-ramaphosa-promises-two-million-jobs-for-youth-in-the-next-10-years/[Accessed 15 10 2019].

Malada, B. 2018. Ramaphosa's New Dawn: Embrace ambition. [Online] Available at: https://www.news24.com/Columnists/GuestColumn/ramaphosas-new-dawn-embrace-ambition-20180624 [Accessed 02 10 2019].

Marrian, N. 2019. Ramaphosa's SONA outlines seven priorities for sixth administration. [Online] Available at: https://mg.co.za/article/2019-06-20-ramaphosas-sona-outlines-seven-priorities-for-sixth-administration [Accessed 11 10 2019].

Maserumule, M.H. 2011. Good governance in the New Partnership for Africa's Development (NEPAD): A public administration perspective. Unpublished PhD Thesis. Pretoria: University of South Africa.

Maserumule, M.H. 2015. Engaged scholarship and liberatory science: A Professoriate, Mount Grace, and SAAPAM in the Decoloniality Mix. Journal of Public Administration, 50(2). 200-222.

Mathe, T. 2019. SA's GDP slumps to its lowest in a decade. [Online] Available at: https://mg.co.za/article/2019-06-04-sas-gdp-slumps-to-its-lowest-in-a-decade [Accessed 10 10 2019].

Mavuso, S. 2019. Why Cyril Ramphosa's dream of more jobs is just a pipe dream. [Online] Available at: https://www.iol.co.za/news/politics/why-cyril-ramphosas-dream-of-more-jobs-is-just-a-pipe-dream-29856288 [Accessed 10 10 2019].

Maya-Rose, T. 2019. 'New Dawn': Ramaphosa's inauguration leaves many positive for SA's future. [Online] Available at: https://briefly.co.za/30620-new-dawn-ramaphosas-inauguration-leaves-positive-sas-future.html [Accessed 11 10 2019].

Mazama, A. 2003. (ed.) The Afrocentric Paradigm. Trenton: Africa World Press.

Mbola, B. 2009. Global economic crisis hinders ASGISA efforts. [Online] Available at: http://www.sanews.gov. za/south-africa/global-economic-crisis-hinders-asgisa-efforts [Accessed 09 10 2019].

Menon, S. & Mkentane, L. 2019. Cyril Ramaphosa faces surging unemployment problem. [Online] Available at: https://www.businesslive.co.za/bd/economy/2019-07-30-cyril-ramaphosa-faces-surging-unemployment-problem/ [Accessed 08 10 2019].

Mkabela, Q. 2005. Using the Afrocentric method in researching indigenous African.. The Qualitative Report, 10(1), pp. 178-89.

Modise, K. 2019. Euphoria around Ramaphosa's new dawn quickly dying, says Mcebisi Jonas. [Online] Available at: https://ewn.co.za/2019/08/14/euphoria-around-ramaphosa-s-new-dawn-quickly-dying-says-mcebisi-jonas. [Accessed 13 10 2019].

Modupe, D. 2003. The Afrocentric philosophical perspective: Narrative outline.

In: Mazama, A. (ed.) The Afrocentric Paradigm. Trenton: Africa World Press.

Mofokeng, N. 2019. Opinion: Ramaphosa's 'New Dawn' has been a fallacy from the beginning. [Online] Available at: https://www.sapeople.com/2019/08/09/opinion-ramaphosas-new-dawn-has-been-a-fallacy-from-the-beginning/ [Accessed 10 10 2019].

Morris, E. 2013. The National Development Plan (NDP): the current state of play. [Online] Available at: http://hsf.org. za/resource-centre/hsf-briefs/the-national-developmentplan-ndp-the-current-state-of-play. [Accessed 08 10 2019].

Mosala, S., Venter, J. & Bain, E. 2017. South Africa's economic transformation since 1994: What influence has the National Democratic Revolution (NDR) Had?. Rev Black Polit Econ, 44 (3-4) 327-340.

Mostert, J.W. 2015. Radical economic transformation and inclusive growth: A provincial perspective. [Online] Available at: file:///C:/Users/201521803/AppData/Local/Packages/Microsoft.MicrosoftEdge_8wekyb3d8bbwe/TempState/Downloads/essa_3320.pdf [Accessed 07 07 2019].

Muller, M. 2019. More to SA's economic woes than Zuma years. [Online] Available at: https://www.sowetanlive.co.za/sundayworld/lifestyle/talk/2019-08-14-more-to-sas-economic-woes-than-zuma-years/ [Accessed 05 10 2019].

Mutize, M. & Gosseland, S. 2017. White monopoly capital': an excuse to avoid South Africa's real problems [27 March 2017]. Braamfontein: South Africa: The Conversation Africa..

Ndlovu-Gatsheni, S. 2018. Epistemic Freedom in Africa. London: Taylor & Francis..

NDP, 2019. The National Development Plan. [Online] Available at: https://nationalplanningcommission.wordpress.com/the-national-development-plan/ [Accessed 12 10 2019].

Ngcobo, K. 2019. VIDEOS: #PeoplesInauguration hailed as a period of renewal. [Online] Available at: https://www.iol.co.za/news/politics/videos-peoplesinauguration-hailed-as-a-period-of-renewal-24009973 [Accessed 13 10 2019].

Nicolson, G. 2019. Ramaphosa cuts Cabinet from 36 to 28 ministers, half of whom are women. [Online] Available at: https://www.dailymaverick.co.za/article/2019-05-29-ramaphosa-cuts-cabinet-from-36-to-28-ministers-half-of-whom-are-women/ [Accessed 10 10 2019].

Nkanjeni, U. 2019. South Africans think corruption increased during Ramaphosa's first six months as president: Report. [Online] Available at: https://www.timeslive.co.za/news/south-africa/2019-08-19-south-africans-think-corruption-increased-during-ramaphosas-first-six-months-as-president-report/ [Accessed 09 10 2019].

NPC, 2012. National Development Plan - Vision 2030. Pretoria: National

Planning Commission.

Onishi, N. & De-Greef, K. 2019. South Africa's President Reappoints Deputy Accused of Graft. [Online] Available at: https://www.nytimes.com/2019/05/29/world/africa/ramaphosa-reappoints-mabuza-south-africa-corruption.html[Accessed 09 10 2019].

Oosthuizen, M. 2016. Why South Africa can't deliver on the social contract set out in its constitution [21 November 2016]. Braamfontein, South Africa: The Conversation Africa.

Owusu-Ansah, F. & Mji, G. 2013. African indigenous knowledge and research.. African Journal of Disability, 2(1): 1-5.

Payne, S. 2019. As Ramaphosa talks bullet trains, Mbalula set to focus on putting Metrorail back on track. [Online] Available at: https://www.dailymaverick.co.za/article/2019-06-21-as-ramaphosa-talks-bullet-trains-mbalula-set-to-focus-on-putting-metrorail-back-on-track/ [Accessed 10 10 2019].

Quintal, G. & Mailovich, C. 2019. Cyril's cabinet compromise. [Online] Available at: https://www.businesslive.co.za/fm/features/2019-06-06-cyrils-cabinet-compromise/ [Accessed 10 10 2019].

Ramorei, K. 2019. Ramaphosa warns South Africans to prepare for mass job losses. [Online] Available at: https://sadcnews.org/2019/07/24/ramaphosa-warns-south-africans-to-prepare-for-mass-job-losses/ [Accessed 09 10 2019].

Rapanyane, M.B. 2018. South Africa's foreign policy towards Israel within the context of the Palestinean question, (1999-2018), Mankweng, University of Limpopo: Unpublished Hons Mini-Dissertation.

Rapanyane, M.B. & Ngoepe, C.C. 2019. The impact of Illicit Financial Flows on the South African political economy under Jacob Zuma, 2009–2018. Journal of Public Affairs.

Shai, K.B. 2017. South African state capture: A symbiotic affair between business and state going bad (?). Insight on Africa, 9(1), pp. 62-75.

Shai, K.B. 2019. A critical analysis of the ANC's christianity driven morality as political theology through the lens of Ahmed Kathrada. UBUNTU: Journal of Conflict and Social Transformation, 8 (1): 121-135.

Sibanda, O & Lekubu, B. 2019. Hands off Zondo – the commission is worth every cent. [Online] Available at: https://www.dailymaverick.co.za/article/2019-10-07-hands-off-zondo-the-commission-is-worth-every-cent/ [Accessed 10 10 2019].

Sidiropoulos, E. 2018. A new dawn in South Africa. [Online] Available at: https://saiia.org.za/research/a-new-dawn-in-south-africa/ [Accessed 11 10 2019].

Smit, S. 2019. Unemployment rate at 29% — StatsSA. [Online] Available at: https://mg.co.za/article/2019-07-30-unemployment-rate-at-29-statssa [Accessed

15 10 2019].

Steyn, L. 2018. Budget 2018 is Zuma's costly legacy. [Online] Available at: https://mg.co.za/article/2018-02-23-budget-2018-is-zumas-costly-legacy [Accessed 08 10 2019].

The-Presidency, 2019. President Cyril Ramaphosa: State of the Nation Address 2019. [Online] Available at: https://www.gov.za/speeches/2SONA2019 [Accessed 10 10 2019].

Van-Diemen, E. 2019. It's not his dream, it's the people's dream' - Magashule defends Ramaphosa's SONA high hopes. [Online] Available at: https://www.news24.com/SouthAfrica/News/its-not-his-dream-its-the-peoples-dream-magashule-defends-ramaphosas-sona-high-hopes-20190621 [Accessed 10 10 2019].

Van-Zyl, G. 2018. Julius Malema: "The EFF is in charge — the ANC is following us.". [Online] Available at: https://www.biznews.com/undictated/2018/08/20/malema-eff-charge-anc-following-us [Accessed 09 10 2019].

Von-Holdt, K. 2019. The political economy of corruption: elite-formatin, factions and violence. [Online] Available at: https://docs.wixstatic.com/ugd/de7bea_0590611beee14069a0e98f83dd26e9ae.pdf [Accessed 09 10 2019].

Wallis, M. 1995. The problem of bureaucratic administration. In: Fitzgerald, P. McLennan, A. & Munslow, F. (eds). Managing Sustainable Development in South Africa. Cape Town: Oxford University Press.

Writer, S. 2019. What business wants from Ramaphosa's State of the Nation address. [Online] Available at: https://businesstech.co.za/news/business/324247/what-business-wants-from-ramaphosas-state-of-the-nation-address/ [Accessed 13 10 2019].

Chapter Nine

The arrogance of *"entitlement"* to sustain ZANU-PF's hold onto power as a liberation political party

Katija Khan

Introduction

The Zimbabwean situation is unique and interesting at the same time, due to the shifts that the liberation movements under went just before the 1980 independence and soon after the war of liberation. Nowhere in Southern Africa is the memory of the liberation struggle being kept alive and guarded in quite the same way as in the case of ZANU-PF of Zimbabwe. ZANU-PF and ZAPU were the leading liberation movements that drew credit for wedging the war that pressured for talks in 1979. The two movements tried a unity government at independence which failed to work. The idea was that ZANU-PF and ZAPU were entitled to leadership and control of the country since they had been visibly instrumental in forcing for the peace settlement and the resultant independence to the country and its people. This conceptualization of entitlement was the reason for the brief civil conflict between the two parties soon after the watershed elections. The civil war was then averted with the signing of the Unity Accord of 1987 which brought the two parties together to become one. Soon after the Unity Accord, veterans of the two liberation movements became one and started claiming entitlement to resources and leadership for life.

The feeling of entitlement got so deep seated from that moment moving into the history of ZANU-PF leadership till today. The fact that they 'liberated the country from the colonial powers has become a form of lifelong entitlement to the country ruler-ship and any attempt to change the government is viewed as regime change meant to give the country back to its colonial masters. The feeling of entitlement has been raised to levels such that any cases of mis-governance, corruption and poor policies should not be raised to justify change of government. This research paper intends to chronicle the challenges that this notion of entitlement has ushered to the country thereby taking a once breadbasket country to a basket case due to the plunder by a few. The catch word used by ZANU-PF is that *"ndisu takasunungura Nyika"*, (we are the ones who liberated the country), and therefore we deserve endless respect. The ambiguity towards full democracy can be seen as rooted in this liberation political culture.

Involvement in the struggle

Liberation movements in Southern Africa represent a history of armed struggle which is simultaneously emancipatory seeking to free oppressed peoples from the chains of the past and from the social and economic deprivations of the present. Due to this notion the Liberation Movements moved to install a repressive system premised on the excuse that because of liberation credentials, the struggle's elites claim for themselves the right to interpret the will of the people.

The ability to define and explain the legacies of the liberation struggle has become a political discourse that underlines the dominance of the ZANU-PF party. The liberation legacy articulation by the party leadership helps define the legitimacy of the past in a discourse of 'insiders versus outsiders'. This discourse has a temporal element, in which the nation is articulated as being in a permanent state of anti-colonial war (Raftopoulos, 2009: 213). In this discourse, the struggle, and the principles of the struggle, are not a thing of the past; rather the principles of the struggle are in a continuous process of adaptation to contemporary challenges or 'attacks' levelled against the sovereignty of the Zimbabwean nation. In the post-war consolidation of ZANU as the dominate legitimate political force in Zimbabwe, an imagery of the liberation war soldier-heroes came to hold a symbolic meaning, as the political elite claimed that participation in the liberation war was the only valid political currency. Despite early overtures towards national unity and reconciliation, according to Raftopoulos (2003: 220), this discourse of political legitimacy entailed generational, racial and class tensions that during the 1990s and 2000s laid the foundation for the formulation of a political project with a narrow interpretation of the history of the liberation war: what Ranger has called 'patriotic history' (Raftopoulos, 2004; Ranger, 2004).

According to Moyo & Yeros (2005) as expressed by the ANC in 1998, "transformation of the state entails, first and foremost, extending the power of the National Liberation Movements (NLM) over all levers of power: the army, the police, the bureaucracy, intelligence structures, the judiciary, the parastatals, and agencies such as regulatory bodies, the public broadcaster, the central bank and so on" (ANC 1998). In essence, the National Democratic Revolution (NDR) prescribes a project of the revolutionary party exercising a political monopoly, justifying this in quasi-scientific terms. It is a prescription which has allowed some analysts to go overboard and to describe the ANC as totalitarian, even though in practice the party's capacity to impose its will on society at large is severely compromised (by, *inter alia*, the power of large-scale capital, dissident popular forces, and not least, the Constitution). Nonetheless, notionally the ANC's strategy of extending its reach over all "levers of power" is revolutionary, and deeply at odds with the notions of separation of powers and constitutional supremacy that are embedded in the Constitution.

They may not explicitly subscribe to the theory of the NDR, but both ZANU-PF and SWAPO embrace the values and practice of "transformation" and the theory of state power which accompanies it, at considerable cost to democratic values (Raftopoulos, 2006).

The post-colonial positioning of the ZANU-PF government as the legitimate leaders and protectors of the nation based on their liberation war 'credentials' was an integral part of the nation-building project after 1980. Norma Kriger has argued that immediately after independence, the symbolic status of the liberation war became "an important emotional symbol and source of legitimacy for the governing élite" (Kriger, 1995:139), and that the way in which the regime constructed symbols of national identity out of the liberation war was a testament to their "commitment to hierarchy, bureaucratic control, and top-down decision-making" (Kriger, 1995:145–146). Kriger has developed this argument by showing how liberation struggle credentials have been important in internal rivalries within ZANU-PF (Kriger, 2006).

War cabinet

At independence, the government was forced to be inclusive of all the parties that had participated and gained some seats in parliament. This was part of the prescriptions from the negotiated settlement in Lancaster. As the new Zimbabwean Prime Minister, Robert Mugabe announced a Cabinet designed to bring together both wings of the Patriotic Front alliance, reassure the country's white minority, and foster unity within his Zimbabwe African National Union Party, as reported by the *Monitor correspondent*, Gary Thatcher in 1980. The appointment of whites from the Rhodesian Front and some members of ZAPU was hailed as a sign of reconciliation and development on the part of ZANU-PF ideology.

There were 23 appointments made to form the first post-colonial cabinet after the 2nd Chimurenga that brought independence to Zimbabwe. Supporters of Mugabe's ZANU party were allocated more than 70% of the appointments with 16 Cabinet seats. Mugabe retained the defense portfolio for himself but made two key appointments to reassure whites. David Smith of the all-white Rhodesian Front was named secretary of commerce and industry, and another white, Denis Norman, was given the post of agriculture minister. He was expected to keep the commercial agricultural economy prosperous while redistributing some acreage to land-hungry African peasants. Joshua Nkomo, another liberation war hero, was given increased powers over the country's police forces as Home Affairs minister. His Zimbabwe African Peoples Union party was given four posts in the 23-member Cabinet. There was only one woman, Teurai Nhongo, who was given a full Cabinet post, as minister of youth, sport, and recreation. All in all, 21 cabinet posts went to former liberation war heroes or people who had associated themselves with radical nationalism which gave a full picture of a war cabinet. The picture of the 1st cabinet indicated how war time heroes were being paid to steer the first government after independence. It gave the picture of entitlement, the *Chinhu Chedu* mentality (Our Thing mentality).

Militarization of government institutions

A militarised economy system implies a penetration of the military ethos into society and the value system of its governing elite. Robert Mugabe, as president of Zimbabwe seemed to have at some point borrowed heavily from the success of the "Asian Tigers". Mugabe was quick to repeat the Indonesian script where, during the 20-year reign of Suharto, the military ensured that government policy followed a path that the military leadership deemed fit. In the first two decades of Suharto's rule, Indonesia experienced rapid industrialisation and economic growth. His almost unquestioned authority over Indonesian affairs slipped dramatically when the Asian financial crisis lowered Indonesians' standards of living and rattled his support among the nation's military, political and civil society institutions.

Suharto was strongly supported by most of the military establishment. His government owned more than 164 enterprises and administered prices on several basic goods, including fuel, staple rice, and electricity, just like Zimbabwe.

All state institutions in Zimbabwe started to be militarized by appointments of former members of the military or liberation heroes to ensure all policies were natured and implemented the ZANU-PF way. Institutions that were affected stretch from legal appointments, parastatals, key arms of the government and all other extended state formations. This was done through an opaque process resulting in critical organisations and services' ownership passing directly to politically connected people. What frightened the public most is not only the military heading institutions but the ruling elite's strong craving for immediate gratification and open denial of qualified civilians from running the show. This tendency ended up despoiling the nation in the name of guaranteeing the commander-in-chief's stay at the helm.

A retired colonel was picked to head the Grain Marketing Board and an Air Force officer was send to the National Railways of Zimbabwe (NRZ). A serving brigadier took reigns at the Sports and Recreation Commission, a situation widely viewed as military encroachment onto social life. Government introduced Operation Maguta where military personnel took over some of the farms previously run by the Agricultural and Rural Development Authority in an effort to boost declining agricultural production.

Laws inconsistent with the Constitution are unconstitutional (Linington, 2012). In practice, while legal forms prevail, the substance of constitutionalism was being subverted by ZANU-PF's manipulation of the judiciary, and the appointment to the Constitutional Court of judges who are biased in favour of the long-ruling party (Southall, 2013: 148–150).

Analysts would be right to say that this behaviour reinforced the notion that ZANU-PF has yet to wean itself from the politics of the liberation struggle and transform from a liberation movement to a modern civilian government. It can also be viewed as a reflection of deep-seated anxiety associated with fears for the future by the ruling elite after past populist policies pushed the economy to the precipice.

Capture of state resources

While the terminology *favoured* is different, during the Mugabe government, a gospel of "indigenization" was effectively pushed as a predatory version of the ideology of the "developmental state". The ZANU-PF manifesto in the 2000 general elections was titled *Taking Back the Economy*, which the party proclaimed was designed to empower the indigenous people of Zimbabwe by enabling them to fully own their country's "God-given natural resources", anchored in a strategy of transferring to local entities at least a 51 per cent controlling equity in all existing foreign-owned businesses. Written in terms of anti-imperialism, national sovereignty, patriotism and national liberation, the manifesto proclaimed its commitments to the state driving the re-capacitation of the economy in the interests of "broad-based empowerment" (ZANU-PF 2013). Suffice it to say that it was designed to appeal to the ordinary, impoverished Zimbabwean, its programme of popular empowerment wholly sidestepping the awkward issue of the ZANU-PF elite's massive gains from the seizure of the country's most valuable resources, from land to diamonds, and henceforth, the party hopes, also from industry and finance. In summary, the whole thread and mantra of empowerment was a front played to allow the ZANU-PF big wigs to have uncensored access to state resources.

The appeal of ZANU-PF to the voters was clearly "populist", if populism is taken as an ideology promoted by an elite to "pit a virtuous and homogeneous people against a set of elites and dangerous 'others' who (are) together depicted as depriving (or attempting to deprive) the sovereign people of their rights, values, prosperity, identity and voice" (Albertazzi & MacDonnell, 2008: 16). Often appropriating Africanist themes, it promotes an agenda which identifies the interests of its driving elites with those of the people, overlooking exploitative relations which may occur between them, and proclaiming that democracy must reflect the undiluted will of the nation.

Partisan land re-distribution

Land has been a source of political conflict in Zimbabwe since colonization, when the country was known as Rhodesia, both within indigenous black communities and especially between white settlers and the black rural communities. Under British colonial rule and under the white minority government that in 1965 unilaterally declared its independence from Britain, white Rhodesians seized control of the vast majority of good agricultural land, leaving black peasants to scrape a living from marginal "tribal reserves."

Mugabe designated his post-2000 land reforms as the "Third Chimurenga", claiming historical continuities with the wars of primary resistance against colonialism in the 1890s (the "First Chimurenga"), and the war for liberation of the 1960s and 1970s (the "Second Chimurenga"). This interpretation served two purposes. First, identifying the 1987 incorporation of ZAPU into ZANU-PF as the consummation of national unity, projecting ZANU-PF as the ultimate embodiment of the nation (Mugabe, 1989). It followed, then, that when the MDC arose to challenge the ruling party, it was reviled as illegitimate, treacherous and as being "outside of" the nation. Second, the presentation of politics (notably land reform) as war enabled those opposed to ZANU-PF's initiatives to be depicted as enemies rather than simply opponents, this implicitly justified any form of violence against them. Furthermore, the third Chimurenga discourse relies on the antagonistic language of war, depicting political opponents as enemies or 'sell-outs' thus justifying violent punishment, as during the liberation war (Christiansen, 2004:78–81). In the early 2000s the relative political inexperience of the MDC was utilised by the ZANU-PF government to depict the MDC in this fashion. An example of this was an incident where leaders of the MDC were shown on CNN receiving cheques from white farmers, who at the time were under attack in the Third Chimurenga land occupations. This footage was turned into government propaganda, as proof of MDC's 'sell-out' status, having literally taken money from the hands of the white colonists (Willems, 2005).

Here, the legacy of the liberation struggle takes an important place, as cultural pride is attached to the anti-colonial struggle in a temporal construct in which the nation is narrated as rooted in a glorious pre-colonial past, only fully realised in the succession of anti-colonial struggles. Thus, defining 'precolonial culture' and the impact of colonial rule on culture is at the centre of the narrative of the nation. That which was lost during the colonial period, the gains of the liberation struggle, and the legacies of the war itself, are therefore important defining elements in the cultural construction of the nation.

The need for land reform in Zimbabwe is something that was fully acknowledged by all including representatives of the Commercial farmers' Union (CFU). History can reveal that colonial policies of land expropriation gave a few thousand white farmers ownership of huge tracts of arable land. It was always reported in the media that about 4,500 large-scale commercial farmers held close to 80 percent of the total land when the fast track program was instituted. This reality was revealed against a statistic of more than one million black families struggling in crowded, arid "communal areas. Farm workers, many of whom were of foreign descent, had little or no access to land of their own, and were also vulnerable to arbitrary eviction from their tied accommodation. Many poor and middle-income black people in urban areas, squeezed by rocketing food and transport price hikes and growing unemployment since the mid-1990s, saw land as an alternative source of income and food security. Many land restitution claims relating to forced removals during the era of the white government were still not addressed. These factors created a significant land hunger in Zimbabwe.

According to media reports during the time and many witnesses interviewed by Human Rights Watch, the process of land distribution itself raised serious concerns. The first problem identified was the ZANU-PF party-political control of access to the forms for applying for land and partisan discrimination in the allocation of plots. The second was the key role of the war veterans' ZANU-PF militias in distributing and allocating land, the same militias were responsible for violence and intimidation against many who applied for plots but were dimmed to be not full members of the ruling party. There was a general exclusion of farm workers from the redistribution of land acquired during the process. Although there was an official structure for allocating land through the civil service and elected officials, in many cases this system was superseded by informal processes governed by the war veterans, who required for one to demonstrate loyalty to ZANU-PF before allocation of a plot. Working in concert with the ruling party militias, the police and army were identified as coordinating some of the land occupations.

Rigging of general elections

If you talk to professors of African history, they will tell you that there has never been a liberation movement in Southern Africa that has willingly given up power through the ballot box. Or to quote Stalin; "It's not the people who vote that count, it's the people who count the votes that matter." (Chris Bateman, August 2, 2018)

Constitutional democracy requires more than a formal adherence by political actors to the text of the Constitution, demanding commitment to constitutional ideals. It implies that the Constitution guarantees the democratic rights of all citizens, balances majority against individual rights, and sets up obstacles to arbitrary rule by promoting the rule of law and by specifying an appropriate separation of powers between the executive, legislature and judiciary. The Zimbabwean election went into meltdown with accusations of a rigged election.

Peter Fabricius writing in the *Daily Maverick* interviewed Tendai Biti, strong member of the MDC Alliance.

> "We're going to fight this," Tendai Biti said grimly after the Zimbabwe Election Commission (ZEC) announced a landslide victory for the ruling ZANU-PF in Monday's parliamentary elections. "The fascists are trying

to steal this election, but we won't accept it," said veteran opposition leader Biti, who is one of the co-leaders of the seven-party Movement for Democratic Change Alliance (MDC-Alliance) coalition which contested the presidential and parliamentary poll. "Our data shows we have won by 61%; Nelson Chamisa has won 61% of the votes. If you win by this much in the presidential elections – for instance in Masvingo (province) where Chamisa won overwhelmingly but hardly won any parliamentary seats – something is wrong. People don't vote for a presidential candidate of one party and not for the MPs of that party. So it's called cheating."

According to Tendai Biti, MDC A election monitors and observers had picked and tallied voting statistics from each polling station which showed that the party had been winning in most of the polling stations. EU election observers tentatively cited pre-election bias of the state media, the party's abuse of state resources and some voter intimidation. They followed this up with their observers' report which was published after the elections. The mission leader, Elmar Brok, cited several reasons for this assessment, including the clear bias of the state media in favour of ZANU-PF, that party's abuse of state resources and instances of intimidation of voters. But, as with other election missions, the EU restricted themselves to only commenting later on the vote-counting.

The results of 2018 general elections produced a contested outcome in the same way that 2008 had shown. There are allegations and indications that Mugabe later admitted that they lost the 2008 election even though the party did not give up power. The story of the GNU of 2008 brokered by Thabo Mbeki of South Africa might just be a good indicator that things failed to work for ZANU-PF because the electorate did not uphold ZANU-PF claim to have won.

The ZANU-PF party is on record pronouncing how they viewed the ascendance of any other party into power in Zimbabwe other than themselves. During the time of Robert Mugabe, the army always stated they would never salute anyone who didn't go war. They even said the nation would never be surrendered to anyone outside ZANU-PF on the pretext of voting saying *Nyika yakauya ne gidi haiende ne pen* which means (the country which was won by the gun cannot be surrendered by a pen, meaning an X in the voting system of democracy). The military has always been seen to be in firm alliance with ZANU-PF, ready to step in if its rule is threatened. This was confirmed on November 17 in 2017 when the army removed Robert Mugabe through a soft coup that was sold as a non-coup. This confirms the fact that ZANU-PF and the army will never allow any other person outside their structures to take over leadership of the country, with or without elections. The democratic picture that ZANU-PF tries to paint by maintaining election dates remains a façade to allude the international community. No election will ever be fair with this liberation movement still in power. Zimbabwe's military-economic élite, a new capitalist class at an early stage, will not be removed just with elections.

Conclusion

National liberation will forever be viewed as both the just and historically necessary conclusion to any struggle between 'the people' and the forces of racism and colonialism. This has two implications. First, the national liberation movements, whatever venial sins they commit, are the righteous. They do not merely represent the masses but in a sense they are the masses, and as such they cannot really be wrong. Second, according to the same theology, their coming to power represents the end of a process. No further group can succeed them for that would mean that the masses, the forces of righteousness, had been overthrown.

If constitutional rule is to survive and advance in Southern Africa, it will need the support of counter-elites and wider society to contest the repressive components of liberation movement culture in order to secure the freedoms for which the liberation movements themselves claim to have fought. Liberation movements' predisposition to exclusive nationalism, defining themselves as representatives of fused conceptions of "the nation" and "the people", reinforce majoritarian conceptions of democracy, and hence are at odds with central tenets of constitutionalism and modern democracy.

References

Alexander, J., McGregor, J. & Ranger, T. 2000. Violence and Memory, One Hundred Years in the 'Dark Forests' of Matabeleland. Oxford: James Currey.

Alexander, J., McGregor, J. & Tendi, B. 2017. The transnational histories of Southern African liberation movements: An introduction. Journal of Southern African Studies, 43:1: 1-12, DOI: 10.1080/03057070.2017.1278982

Campbell, H. 2003. Reclaiming Zimbabwe: The Exhaustion of the Patriarchal Model of Liberation. Trenton: Africa World Press.

Christiansen, L.B. 2004. Tales of the nation: feminist nationalism or patriotic history? Defining national history and identity in Zimbabwe. Research Report no. 132. Uppsala: Nordic Africa Institute.

Christiansen, L.B. 2009. In our culture": How debates about Zimbabwe's domestic violence law became a "culture struggle". NORA Nordic Journal of Feminist and Gender Research 17(3).

Johnson, R.W. 2001. The final struggle is to stay in power, Focus, 25, online: http://hsf.org.za/resource-centre/focus/issue-25–first-quarter-2002/the-final-struggle-is-to-stay-in-power

Kössler, R. 2010. Images of history and the nation: Namibia and Zimbabwe compared, South African Historical Journal, 62(1): 29–53.

Kriger, N. 2006. From patriotic memories to 'patriotic history' in Zimbabwe,

1990– 2005", Third World Quarterly, 27(6).

Kriger, N. J. 1995. The politics of creating national heroes: The search for political legitimacy and national identity, In: Bhebe, N. & Ranger, T.O. (eds). Soldiers in Zimbabwe's Liberation War. London: James Currey.

Mandaza, I. 1986. The state and politics in the post-settler situation, In: Mandaza, I. (ed.) Zimbabwe: The Political Economy of Transition, 1980–1986. Dakar: Codesria; Harare: Jongwe Press.

Moyo, S. & Yeros, P. 2005. Land occupations and land reform in Zimbabwe: Towards the national democratic revolution, In: Moyo, S. & Yeros, P. (eds). The Resurgence of Rural Movements in Africa, Asia and Latin America, London: Zed Press, 44–77.

Mugabe, R. 1989. The Unity Accord: Its promise for the future. In: Banana, C. (ed.) Turmoil and Tenacity: Zimbabwe 1890–1990. Harare: The College Press, 336–359.

Mugabe, R. 2001. Inside the Third Chimurenga. Our Land is our Prosperity. Harare: Department of Information and Publicity.

Raftopoulos, B. 2004. Nation, race and history in Zimbabwean politics. In: Raftopoulos, B. & Savage, T. (eds). Injustice and Political Reconciliation. Cape Town: Institute for Justice and Reconciliation.

Raftopoulos, B. 2009. The Crisis in Zimbabwe, 1998–2008. In: Raftopoulos, B. & Mlambo, A. (eds). Becoming Zimbabwe. A History from the Pre-colonial Period to 2008. Harare: Weaver Press.

Ranger, T. 2004. Nationalist historiography, patriotic history, and the history of the nation: The struggle over the past in Zimbabwe. Journal of Southern African Studies, 30(2): 215–234.

Chapter Ten

Use of public media in attacking the ghost of 'regime change' agenda in defense of liberation movements in Southern Africa: ZANU-PF case

Josephat Mutangadura

Introduction

> As the international community celebrated World Media Day on 3 May 2003, Zimbabweans in the media profession and other concerned citizens agreed to observe the occasion with a carefully chosen theme: *"the media we have is not the media we need."*

Empirical research on mass media effects in the modern era began in the 1930s, partly motivated by Hitler's and Mussolini's seemingly effective use of media in their propaganda and the simultaneous influence on the political front. Early research on media was convinced that media effect was capable of brainwashing people through injecting them with propaganda messages. Assuming this model of media effects were true, the power of media would certainly have a huge negative influence on its consumers. This theory was called hypodermic needle theory or the magic bullet theory. The first large-scale studies found that the mass media of radio and print had relatively minor direct effects on people's voting intentions (Lazarsfeld, Berelson & Gaudet, 1944; Berelson, Lazarsfeld & McPhee, 1954). Studies conducted in 1940 and 1948 established that the media seemed mainly to reinforce voters' prior dispositions and not necessarily change their voting intentions. This was partly because few respondents changed their voting intentions at all, and partly because people exposed themselves to media that shared their prior views. Similarly, experimental studies showed that while propaganda movies did make people learn facts, they did not often significantly change attitudes (Hovland, Lumsdaine & She¢eld, 1949).

After carefully sorting out the available evidence in 1960, Klapper (1960) concluded that a mass communication far more frequently acted as an agent of reinforcement than as an agent of change". To the disappointment of many media researchers, minimal effects of media on voting became the conventional wisdom. In response to these findings, researchers developed new theories of media influence that do not rely on people receiving information that connects with their prior beliefs: agenda setting, priming, and framing. Framing theory is instead based on the assumption that how an issue is characterized in news reports can have an influence on how it is understood by audiences. Whereas agenda setting and priming influence what people think about, framing influences how they think about it. Media studies of framing often refer to Gofman (1974) and Kahneman and Tversky (1984), but the connections are rather loose. A large part of framing involves the selective inclusion or omission of exactly the type of facts that would be valuable for political accountability. This type of selective inclusion and omission of facts has been extensively analyzed by economists under the label media bias (Baron, 2006; Mullainathan & Shleifer, 2005; Gentzkow & Shapiro, 2006). In this study, ZANU-PF seemed to have been using public media to agenda set and to also frame the media reportage and news items as shall be seen in the various topics discussed below.

Overview of the Zimbabwean political discourse scenario

Ideally, the media should serve essential roles in any democracy. The primary purpose of media should be to inform the public, providing them with the information needed to make thoughtful decisions about political leadership and decision making. The media always act as a watchdog on actions emanating from political leadership. The media can also set the agenda for public debates on issues and provide a forum for political expression. They should also facilitate community building by helping people to find common causes, identify civic groups, and work toward solutions to societal problems. The situation we find in Zimbabwe under the leadership and ideology of ZANU-PF government has been such that restrictions of spaces or zones of communication have been a way to manage challenges to state control and legitimacy against perceived internal and external enemies. In the first period after independence, the ZANU-PF ideology was to create and manage communication control in order to limit free expression so as to manage political discourse. In their attempt to protect and achieve its ideology, ZANU-PF developed a three-pronged strategy summarized by Mazango (2005: 98) as; the centralization of an enhanced Information Ministry in the President's office to lead a new and invigorated project of media control, at the same time articulating a coherent defense of state policy. The second strategy was the use of monopoly broadcasting as a tool to legitimize ruling party hegemony and the last and final tactic was the promulgation of harsh media laws in combination with other extra-legal tactics to control journalists and the private press, while at the same time directing the state owned newspaper oligopoly to serve government propaganda objectives more patriotically. The result has been polarisation of ideas and a clear shrinkage of alternative voices and of political space in the country. The government of ZANU-PF does not seem to worry about the negativity this has had on the functioning and development of media in the country. Their pre-occupation has and remains directed at defending the rule of the liberation movement as the only legitimate system. Any other information to the contrary is viewed as a regime change agenda being sponsored to defeat the will of the people as espoused in the liberation ideology.

Brief history of media and politics

The media is often referred to as "The Fourth Estate" with the important function of being "the press" and serving as the eyes and ears of the public. The traditional print media reporting has been viewed over time as the way to ensure the public gets the real view on the functioning of government and viewpoints of political ideologies of the ruling elite. The news media is a societal or political force or institution whose influence is expected to act in the interest of the public. When the media is functioning well, it should ensure the following essential duties:

1. Holding government leaders accountable to the people.

2. Publicising issues that need attention.

3. Educating citizens so they can make informed decisions, and

4. Connecting people with each other in civil society.

Media that is operating in a conducive environment should lay an important foundation in influencing political discourse. Free and balanced, traditional media (print and broadcast) should foster transparency and the determination of important political discourse. The emergence of new media provides further opportunities for participatory citizenship in political debates.

Assaults on the media in the country can be traced back to colonial times following the unilateral declaration of independence in 1965. Censors resulted in swathes of news stories being removed, and then littering papers with blank pages. This overt censorship was but a new manifestation of a repressive media heritage (Mukasa, 2003). When Ian Smith came to power in early 1965, a new information department together with the Rhodesian Broadcasting Corporation (RBC) shaped government information propaganda to reflect the outlook of the Rhodesian Front (RF). At that time the collision course with both the British government and the nationalists at home led to a conflict of loyalties with almost everyone who disagreed with the RF being branded as 'communist' or 'traitor' (Parker, 1972; Windrich, 1981). A full-scale propaganda campaign to defend unilateral declaration of independence from Britain (UDI) and to project Rhodesia's new image overseas was launched. Domestically, Africans were supplied with 'suitable propaganda' in order to fill the void left by the banning of their leaders, parties and publications under the Law and Order Maintenance Act (LOMA) and the Emergency Powers Act of 1960.

Parallels can be drawn between Rhodesian and current press and broadcasting machinations under ZANU PF. This question arises if one observes the similarity, that the government of today is being driven by the belief that there is a world conspiracy against ZANU-PF's chosen development path and the re-assertion of its independence. Despite the existence of unfriendly press and defamation laws that were occasionally used, the government still exhibits a feeling of fear and mistrust such that no peaceful co-existence between the government and private newspapers can be guaranteed. This has been the norm from the 1990s to this date. The situation began to change in the late 1990s when a number of new independent titles such as The Independent and The Standard began to criticize deficiencies and growing corruption by public office bearers.

Media structures in Zimbabwe

With independence in 1980, the bulk of the surviving nationalist press, especially those published externally, and some of the church publications ironically faded into oblivion while the hitherto colonial press switched its allegiance to a new ruling elite (Mukasa, 2003). The Zimbabwean government subsequently bought the majority of shares in Zimbabwe Newspapers, a company that owned all major newspapers in the country. The government then established the Zimbabwe Mass Media Trust (ZMMT) whose stated role was to promote, through an independent board of non-government individuals, the interests of ordinary Zimbabweans in the national media (ibid). Ostensibly, government wanted to give the impression that they would not be involved in monitoring and mentoring the press on a day to day basis. In reality, ZMMT would be subject to a systemic pattern of government attempts to control and influence the press. At the end of 1980, the new government replaced all the white editors at Zimbabwe Newspapers. Farayi Munyuki became the first black editor of The Herald; Tommy Sithole, The Chronicle; the late Willy Musarurwa took over The Sunday Mail; and Bill Saidi The Sunday News. A government minister, Enos Nkala, did not mince his words when he said white editors were incapable of articulating and supporting a black government (Mukasa, 2003: 177).

In actual fact, the government strongly controls the two main daily newspapers, the *Chronicle* and the *Herald*, whose propagandistic coverage generally favours ZANU-PF and its leadership. The private Alpha Media Holdings group publishes a number of the country's independent papers, including *NewsDay*, the *Standard*, and the *Zimbabwe Independent*. The *Daily News*, published by Associated Newspapers of Zimbabwe, resumed operations in 2011 after being shuttered in 2003 and is generally aligned with the opposition viewpoints. Some foreign newspapers, mainly from South Africa, are available despite a 2012 ZMC directive banning the distribution of unregistered foreign newspapers.

Media legislation

The new constitution developed and enacted in 2013 at the end of the National Unity Government provides for freedom of expression and access to information, though with some limitations. However, an otherwise draconian legal framework continues to inhibit the activities of media, journalism and media houses. The 2002 Access to Information and Protection of Privacy Act (AIPPA) requires all journalists and media companies to register and gives the information minister sweeping powers to decide which publications can operate legally and who is able to work as a journalist. Unlicensed journalists can face criminal charges and a sentence of up to two years in prison. In addition, the Public Order and Security Act (POSA) and the Criminal Law (Codification and Reform) Act severely limit what journalists may publish and proffers harsh penalties including long prison sentences for violators. The 2007 Interception of Communications Act allows officials to intercept telephonic and electronic communications and to monitor their content to prevent a "serious offense" or a "threat to national security." In April 2015, the government announced plans to draft a cybercrime bill, which advocacy groups feared could lead to unchecked surveillance and limitations on free expression online.

ZANU-PF crafted repressive media laws like the Public Order and Security Act (POSA) (2002) adopted from the colonial legislation of the Ian Smith regime called Law and Order Maintenance Act (LOMA). Section 15 of POSA reinforces AIPPA that criminalizes communicating statements 'prejudicial to the state, its interests 'in the absence of reasonable grounds that they are not true.' Section 16 also suppresses freedom of expression by prescribing a jail term of up to a year to people who make statements "knowing or realizing that there is a risk or possibility of engendering feelings of hostility towards, or cause hatred, contempt or ridicule of the President" Before the two laws, which were roundly condemned locally and internationally by human rights and civil society organisations, government had also passed The Broadcasting Services Act in 2001, which closed the broadcasting space and gave ZBC a monopoly. Other laws that stifle press freedom include the Parliamentary Privileges and Immunities Act, Official Secrets Act, the Criminal Law (Codification and Reform) Act (CODE), Official Secrets Act, The Censorship and Entertainment Controls Act (CECA), the Interception of Communications Act (ICA), Copyright and Neighbouring Rights Act, as well as the Defence and Police Acts.

Freedom of the press is restricted in Zimbabwe as the government has not yet aligned media laws with the country's new constitution passed in 2013, and, among other violations, media authorities arbitrarily deny licenses to community radio stations. Journalists face harassment, threats, and arbitrary arrests, and increasingly dire economic conditions continue to cause job losses and financial strain in the media sector. The restrictive legal atmosphere is exacerbated by frequent and hostile rhetoric directed against the media by high-level government officials. In September 2015, Robert Mugabe, as president, accused the press of fomenting discord by spreading lies concerning disputes within Zimbabwe's political leadership, and threatened to more severely curtail their operations. The Information Minister issued similar threats in October of the same year.

The Zimbabwe Media Commission (ZMC) regulates the licensing of publications and journalists. In 2012, the ZMC announced the creation of the 13-member Zimbabwe Media Council, as provided for under the AIPPA. The council was charged with developing codes of conduct for print media and has the power to impose punishments on media houses that transgress the codes. However, chronic underfunding and political interference has greatly constrained its capacity to fulfil this mandate. The independent Voluntary Media Council of Zimbabwe (VMCZ), a self-regulatory body for all types of media that was/is supported by a majority of print outlets, has continued to develop its scope of activities, and has heard numerous formal complaints and adjudicated disputes over media content. In 2015, the council registered nearly two dozen complaints from members of the public.

Government retains its monopoly over broadcasting, with the Zimbabwe Broadcasting Corporation (ZBC) being the sole licensed service provider. The only alternative Zimbabwean voices coming through the airwaves are those that broadcast for a few hours a day on short wave radio stations operated from abroad such as Voice of the People, SW Radio Africa, Studio 7 and Community Radio Zimbabwe. Thus, the national and only broadcaster in Zimbabwe is both state-owned and state-controlled, serving the interests of the ruling party ZANU-PF. Broadcasting licenses have been consistently denied to independent and community radio stations but granted to government-affiliated organizations. It is ironic that independent outlets that dare campaign for issuance of licenses to private operators face harassment and persecution from the authorities. Critics continue to allege that the board of the Broadcasting Authority of Zimbabwe (BAZ), which is responsible for granting radio and television licenses, was illegally appointed in 2009 by the information minister and stacked with loyalists of ZANU-PF. In early 2014, the government began to move forward with a plan to license 25 new community radio stations. In February 2015, the BAZ granted only eight licenses, having considered a pool of nearly two dozen applicants. Media advocacy groups criticized the process for its complexity, political nature, and prohibitively high fees, which had caused several contenders to withdraw; critics of the process also noted that almost all groups that received licenses were linked to current or former government officials or state-owned enterprises.

Professional and media-monitoring organizations such as the Zimbabwe Union of Journalists, the Media Monitoring Project of Zimbabwe, and the local chapter of MISA are also occasionally subject to official pressure.

ZANU-PF and media propaganda

Media institutions are important in all political processes because they are used by controlling powers to mobilize bias. It is beyond doubt that media games and control of the media has played a crucial role in maintaining ZANU-PF in power in Zimbabwe. The continuing challenges faced by the opposition MDC is partly linked to unfavourable rules of access to the media and the party's failure to find an alternative outlet. At the same time, it seems ZANU-PF's endeavour to legitimize itself by hemming in the media has had mixed outcomes.

The beginning of serious propaganda at state media enterprises came in 2000 with the appointment of Jonathan Moyo to head the ministry. As a former university political professor, and astute political observer, (and at one time Mugabe's most celebrated critic) the maverick Moyo's tenure was marked by the attempt to revamp the control of information flow into and from Zimbabwe. His appointment as the Minister of Information and Broadcasting Services turned a new leaf in the media fraternity in Zimbabwe. He retired the old guard in the Ministry so as to build a leaner and meaner machine. The department became responsible for the public relations build-up of the President and all government ministries. Moyo dissolved the Mass Media Trust such that public shares in public newspapers now directly came under government control. A coterie of new laws was passed to re-organise the various media such as the press and broadcasting. Zimpapers titles were restructured with company boards being reshuffled and independent minded editors being shown the door. Business caution was thrown out of the window as state titles were excessively used as government attack dogs on 'enemies of the state' (Mazango, 2003).

The propaganda war was declared through editorials and hard-hitting columns falling under by-lines such as *'Nathaniel Manheru'* in The Herald, *'Tafataona Mahoso'* and *'Lowani Ndlovu'* in The Sunday Mail and *'Mzala Joe'* in The Sunday News. The columns and columnists presented a complex mixture of vitriol and intellectual discourse on pan-Africanism trying to unpack, expose, discredit and smear the opposition, labelling them variously as 'misguided', 'stooges', 'terrorists', 'puppets' and 'sell-outs'. All this was meant to paint ZANU-PF as a liberation party with the people's will at heart.

The state-controlled Zimbabwe Broadcasting Corporation (ZBC) runs the vast majority of broadcast media outlets, which are subject to overt political interference and censorship; ZBC coverage overwhelmingly favours ZANU-PF.

Political interference in the running of the affairs of the state broadcaster and the dismissal of top management became frequent occurrences after Moyo assumed headship. Over a period of eight years the ZBC went through five chief executive officers as the minister tried all else to establish a true stooge. In the aftermath of the election on 29 March 2008, for example, in which Robert Mugabe as the presidential candidate of the ruling party was defeated, the ZANU-PF government removed a number of senior managers of the ZBC, accusing them of not handling the election in a proper manner. The then CEO, Henry Muradzikwa, was fired by the board chairman, Justin Mutasa, as a result of pressure from the permanent secretary in the ministry of information and publicity, George Charamba. Eight senior journalists and producers were also suspended soon afterwards amid accusations that they were sympathetic to the rival (and election winner) Movement for Democratic Change (MDC). The truth is that these members being accused had only tried to be fair and impartial as espoused in the charter of ZBC as a public broadcaster. Editorial independence at the ZBC is non-existent and the broadcaster is de facto run from the ministry.

There were allegations of direct political interference from political figures which resulted in news blackouts and stoppage of programmes which are deemed unsuitable by the party. At times, insiders would say, the minister and the permanent secretary do not even have to give instructions for the banning of certain information, with the journalists resorting to self-censorship and 'sunshine journalism' out of fear of offending the 'big bosses'. MISA Zimbabwe further noted that the ZANU-PF succession fights 'posed serious challenges to media editorial independence, journalism ethics and professionalism.

The next level in the hierarchy of political control at the state broadcaster is that of management. According interviews conducted by Mazango (2005) these management positions are also political appointees and wield a lot of power over employees especially in the news department. There is rumored to be a reference structure is in place from the heads of news to assignment editors, senior reporters, down to chief provincial reporters and reporters (with all higher positions traditionally held by ZANU-PF members or sympathisers). 'Sensitive' or 'controversial' news stories are vetted by the heads of news. The day-to-day final compilation of television and radio news bulletins is supervised by the heads and at times requires clearing by the CEO and the ministry. During the same interviews (ibid) with journalists and other practitioners at the ZBC, the majority pointed out that there is a great deal of interference by ZANU-PF officials which hinders the professional and efficient operations of the ZBC. Politicians often give instructions to managerial staff on their editorial preferences. It is also alleged that the divisions and factionalism within the party play out in the newsrooms. For instance, one journalist spoke of how a minister may phone in and give a directive regarding a story and soon after a permanent secretary will call and give instructions that counteract the initial directive. Politicians will stipulate who to report on and who not to report on.

After compromising the management of the broadcaster, the project went on to restructure the programming set. This stage of propaganda at the ZBC needs to be understood and contextualised within the complex political and economic crisis that engulfed the country from 2000 onwards. The vote against a proposed new constitution in the referendum held in February that year served as the first clear warning sign for the ruling party that its hitherto unquestioned dominance and presumed unassailability was coming under threat. This was followed two years later by general elections in which, for the first time since independence, a new political party (the Movement for Democratic Change, MDC) gained out of 120 seats in parliament and the opposition candidate (Morgan Tsvangirai) nearly won the highly contested presidential vote. Moyo, as the new Minister of Information and Publicity in 2000, made sure programming at ZBC went through fundamental changes.

Moyo introduced and used the 'local content' provision to introduce programmes that were only supportive of ZANU-PF. Many programmes emanating from outside Zimbabwe were taken off the air. In their place, documentaries about the 1970s liberation war and programmes on land reform such as Nhaka Yedu (Our Heritage), National Ethos and the New Farmer/ Murimi Wanhasi/Umlime Walamuhla were introduced and given more and more prominence. All of them focused on issues of land and national identity, an adopted ZAN-PF campaign themes in the presidential and parliamentary elections of 2002 and 2005. These themes ran across all programming formats and genres (for example, children, education, current affairs and gender). This period beats them all as the moment of implicitly propaganda that pushed many people to look for alternative Tv and radio services. The influx of Wiztech free-to-air decoders' and Multichoice subscriptions came through many homes at this time. The 'national identity' project of the ZBC was a politically driven effort by the ruling party in complete disregard of the diverse opinions that Zimbabweans held. The redefinition of Zimbabwean national identity and what it means to be Zimbabwean was narrow and those who did not agree with ZANU-PF's philosophy were labelled as the 'other', 'evil' or as 'sell-outs' representing the interests of the West. Thus, those working in civil society organisations, political opposition parties (in particular the MDC) and white Zimbabweans were either vilified by the state broadcaster or excluded from the airwaves altogether. The ZBC nolonger have any feedback and complaints procedure. In the 1980s, ZBC-TV used to air a programme called Facts and Opinions that gave viewers a platform to raise concerns about the broadcaster. However, this programme was dropped after the transformation of the ZBC beginning in 2000.

Music that was featured on both radio and television also promoted the ruling party's policies. Protest songs from the country's well known artists like Oliver Mtukudzi, Thomas Mapfumo, Lovemore Majaivana, Albert Nyathi and others that had human rights, corruption and abuse of power as their main themes, were blacklisted and replaced with progovernment songs that were supportive of ZANU-PF and the land reform programme and critical of Western leaders, especially then UK Prime Minister Tony Blair and then US President George W. Bush. The government, through the office of the minister of information and publicity, Moyo, commissioned pro-ZANU-PF music albums and jingles that filled the airwaves, leading to a total blackout of other types of music.

Moyo himself, using public funds, promoted the production of a series of albums under the label 'Pax Afro', intended to 'communicate the regime's political messages of a resurrected liberation struggle, ultra-patriotism, land reclamation, anti-colonialism and pan Africanism.' The most prominent of these productions was the 26-track double CD titled Back2Black. A study conducted by the Media Monitoring Project of Zimbabwe (MMPZ) in 2003 showed that one of the propaganda jingles, 'Rambai Makashinga' (Continue Persevering), was being played on average 288 times a day on ZBC's four radio stations, which amounts to 8 640 times per month. On television, the jingle was flighted approximately 72 times a day, which amounts to 2 160 times a month (MMPZ).

In 2012, two new private radio stations - Star FM and ZiFM - commenced operation. Despite initial concerns over their owners' close ties to ZANU-PF, local analysts noted that the stations' news and talk radio content presented a diversity of views. The Broadcasting Services Act bans foreign funding and investment in this capital-intensive sector, making it very difficult for private players to enter the market. Radio broadcasts are currently the main source of information in rural areas. Access to broadcast media in these districts is hampered by deteriorating equipment and a lack of transmission sites. However, Zimbabwe's transition from analog to digital broadcasting has provided an opportunity to upgrade the country's broadcast infrastructure, and in 2015, authorities reached agreements with European and Chinese companies to facilitate improvements. ZANU-PF support base is largely the rural populace and radio is the major source of information media for this target group. Radio Zimbabwe and National FM are more used to spread propaganda to the rural population. Studio 7, a private and opposition sympathetic station is always conscripted so that alternatives views do not reach the rural population for propaganda reasons.

Framing of news reportage in the state media outlets

Framing, often used interchangeably with 'representation,' refers to the way in which news media resort to particular interpretive structures to set particular events within their broader context. A frame in communication or a media frame refers to the words, images, phrases, and presentation styles that a speaker or a media outlet uses when relaying information about an issue or event to an audience (Gamson & Modigliani, 1987; 1989). The chosen frame reveals what the speaker sees as relevant to the topic at hand.

News reporting on Zimbabwe and the articulation of issues and standpoints within sections of the local and international audience has played a central role in shaping an understanding of what can be seen as an unfolding 'drama of democratization' (Shelley, 2001). In Zimbabwe, itself, state control and regulation of the media has loomed large in ZANU-PF's plan to consolidate its slipping power, and popularity especially in the remobilization drive after the threats shown to its legitimacy in the 2000, 2002 and 2008 elections. In a well calculated counter-strategy to legitimize its actions, to regain citizen's loyalties, and, not least, to rebut what it increasingly sees as an international onslaught on the country's sovereignty, the ZANU-PF government, which has been in power since 1980, tried to make itself relevant again by deftly constructing an alternative discourse and rhetoric of national solidarity built around the outstanding goals of the 1970s war of liberation from colonialism (Phimister, 2004; Ranger, 2004).

> The government-controlled media, which include Zimbabwe Newspapers (Zimpapers), the biggest newspaper publisher with two dailies and several prominent weeklies, the New Zimbabwe Inter Africa News Agency (ZIANA), the state news agency, and the Zimbabwe Broadcasting Holdings (ZBH), the monopoly state broadcaster, have been very instrumental in this mission of agenda setting and agenda control. (Mukasa, 2003: 175)

The Herald use of cartoon strips to demonise opposition whilst legitimizing ZANU-PF

The two cartoon strips above have been taken from the Herald newspaper after the 2018 general elections. These elections are still being contested by the main opposition which allege serious rigging. The constitutional court ruled against the MDC challenge and declared Mnangagwa as the winner of the July 30 general elections. The use of cartoon was being used to portray a popular party in ZANU-PF against a 'regime change' sponsored party in the MDC. The implication is that the whole country voted for and endorsed the incumbent leaving MDC as an outsider project that will never be satisfied by any system. ZANU-PF is being presented as a people's party representing the liberation war ethos unlike the MDC which is being sponsored by the West.

This last cartoon has been included here to show how fellow African leaders are portrayed to have lend their support to ZANU-PF. Museveni was invited in April 2019 to officially open the International Trade Fair that is held annually in the 2nd largest city in Zimbabwe. The cartoon is broadcasting his speech as a pointer to the fair trade that is being conscripted by the Sanctions imposed on the country by the West. ZANU-PF is always projecting a picture of a committed government that is being disturbed by the sanctions imposed on its leadership. ZANU-PF cannot just accept that they have failed the country and that the population no-longer trust in its continued leadership.

Pvt Media repression

Autocratic governments try to discredit the private press through attacks linking them to destabilising the country (Ronning & Khupe, 2005: 151):

> "It is characteristic of the relationship between the government and the press in monolithic systems that representatives of the rulers tend to attack the independent press regularly on the basis of two sorts of arguments: either that they represent a divisional threat to national unity and cohesion, or that they purvey slander and lies."

Operating in autocratic environments, such as Zimbabwe, where hegemonic and partisan ruling parties reductively compartmentalize citizens into simplistic binaries of 'patriots' and 'sell-outs' as well as 'supporters' and 'enemies' exerts inordinate pressure on private media journalists (Mazango, 2005: 43). Because of the foregoing polarizations fermented by ZANU- PF, framing of and exposing the Zimbabwean story has largely been through the problematic and subjective lens marked by binaries of 'pro-ruling party' and 'anti- ruling party' reportage. It has been argued that two models of journalism are evident, patriotic versus oppositional journalism (Chuma, 2005). These binaries became quite distinct after the formation of the main opposition party, the Movement for Democratic Change (MDC) in 1999, as well as during the post-2000 land seizures by ZANU- PF and the 2008 financial and economic crisis. ZANU-PF accused the local privately-owned media and international media of being sympathetic to the former white commercial farmers (Willems, 2004).

According to Mano (2005), as the bulk of Zimbabwean editors were socialized to be ideological handmaidens of the ruling ZANU-PF ideology, a good number of well-trained journalists tried to exert their professionalism and journalistic independence. They inevitably suffered consequences for their actions. However, the fact that they tried at all to be independent signaled a new era in the growth and development of the press in independent Zimbabwe. The Zimbabwean media has faced a host of challenges in the last two decades, (Mano 2005:61), not least the formation of the biggest opposition party to give ZANU-PF headaches-the MDC. In addition, a hostile political environment; an unfavourable business environment due to a collapsing economy; the land seizures of farms belonging to former white commercial farmers, rampant corruption and the general discontent among the citizenry over a worsening economy.

In what can be termed a discursive demolition of so-called 'enemies of the state', who are said to be opposed to the nation's collective history as borne out of the 1970s-armed struggle for independence, are constantly labelled and daily vilified (Mazango, 2005: 41). State controlled media consistently lampoons prominent political opponents such as the opposition MDC formed and led by Morgan Tsvangirai, foreign funded civil society organizations, and the independent or non-government owned media as 'instruments of neo-colonialism' and 'shameless surrogates of Western interests', particularly of Britain and the United States. It is conflated that by contesting the legitimacy of government and its policies these entities are opposed to the country's history and independence. They are accused of being used as fronts to disseminate covert anti-Zimbabwe messages in a scheme to instigate regime change so as to take the country back into the yoke of external subjugation. For opposing the ZANU-PF government and inviting the imposition of sanctions on the government blame has masterfully been apportioned on the opposition that they are negating the oneness that makes for national identity and are fomenting social strife and instability in a once peaceful and prosperous country. Through editorials and hard-hitting columns, the public media is always pouring out a complex mixture of vitriol and intellectual discourse on pan-Africanism trying to unpack, expose, discredit and smear the opposition, labelling them variously as 'misguided', 'stooges', 'terrorists', 'puppets' and 'sell-outs'. Earlier in Rhodesia, Ian Smith's government had led a campaign of hatred directed at all opponents who were labelled as 'quislings', 'seedy liberals', 'traitors'or/and 'renegades'.

The notable private newspaper to have emerged post-independence, the Daily News was launched in March 1999. A few weeks before the paper was launched, two journalists, Ray Choto and Mark Chavunduka from another privately owned weekly, The Standard, were arrested and severely tortured by state security agents after they published a story alleging that some senior army officers had been arrested in connection with a coup attempt. Responding to the torture of the two journalists in a live, televised address on Zimbabwe Television (ZTV) on 6 February 1999, the then President, Robert Mugabe said the two scribes deserved it and the torture served them right:

> They (The Standard journalists) had through their deliberate and treasonable act invited that reaction……Any media organisation which wilfully suspends truth necessarily forfeits its right to inform and must not cry foul when extraordinary reaction visits them.

The Daily News became a victim of its own success and easily fell into trouble with the authorities when it published unverified stories, which turned out to be false. Since its launch, in official circles the paper had always been associated with both local and international opposition. Its editor, Geoff Nyarota, on being asked by a journalist on state TV why the paper was riding on the electoral success of the MDC with its anti-government slant responded that many expressed the belief that the MDC was in fact riding on the success of The Daily News in providing a contrary opinion. After having been pressured to shake-off the British shareholding, it did not help that its new proprietor, Strive Masiyiwa, a telecommunications mogul who, a few years back, had dragged the state to the Supreme Court to get a mobile phone license and was now still considered one of ZANU-PF's arch enemies. By refusing to register under AIPPA, The Daily News eventually lost the right to publish altogether and was closed down in 2003. This law together with extra-legal tactics like regular ministerial threats, the bombing of presses, deportation of foreign journalists and arrests of local ones contributed to shrink the media space in the country.

The government of ZANU-PF continued to exploit restrictive laws to harass and punish journalists in 2015. In June, journalist Patrick Chitongo was sentenced to one year in prison for publishing an unregistered newspaper, the *Southern Mirror*, in violation of the AIPPA. In November, authorities arrested photojournalist Anderson Shadreck Manyere for filming clashes between the police and supporters of the Movement for Democratic Change–Tsvangirai (MDC-T), Zimbabwe's main opposition party. He was charged with "participating in a gathering with intent to promote public violence, breaches of the peace or bigotry." The charges were always trumped up, yet the real reason for vilification was to silence any other voice that would go against the state propaganda.

Flow of information in the domestic space has been curtailed by the closing down of independent newspapers such as the Daily News, Daily News on Sunday, The Tribune, and the Weekly Times that once created room for voices outside government. Simultaneously, the banning of foreign journalists has controlled the flow of news from the country to the international public. Besides the odd mention in the sympathetic international press this has left the opposition with no access to an arena necessary to articulate their position.

Conclusions

Ownership and control of the largest share of the media market has allowed the government to dominate spaces of public communication and to control an important instrument of veto. Using strategic timing, the overriding aim has been to side-track criticisms that allege poor governance and human rights abuses by placing land and economic empowerment as the central issues for national debate. Through the ready platform presented by government-controlled media, ruling party-political communicators and political persuaders have denied the opposition an opportunity to air contrary views and, not least, painted them as enemies of the state. Quite naturally, controversial public debates on issues facing the country have been framed using rhetorical strategies that emphasize and prioritize policy goals and policy images consistent with the ZANU-PF manifesto whilst selectively highlighting the opposition's weaknesses.

However, it is undeniable that what remains of the independent press in Zimbabwe exists under an increasingly trying environment governed by harsh media legislation such as the Access to Information and Protection of Privacy Act (AIPPA) and the Public Order and Security Act (POSA) that make the practice of journalism in the country today to be likened to walking a minefield. Such a scenario of seemingly permissible criticism of government amidst strict press regulations reveals contradictions between the authoritarian and the democratic impulses in the political development of the country (Rønning, 2002). The result has been a contraposition of two almost conflicting viewpoints on the country, binary positions that have spurred rigidly contrasting coverage. The implication is that one story on Zimbabwe today is never the whole story. Or put differently, depending on whom you listen to.

References

A comparative analysis of ZBC and private radio stations' coverage of issues: July 13th–August 2nd 2009. Report compiled by the MMPZ during September 2009.

Casper, G. 2000. The benefits of difficult transitions. Democratization, 7(3): 46-62

Catholic Commission for Justice and Peace in Rhodesia (1977) Rhodesia: The Propaganda War, Salisbury.

Charlton, M. 1990. The Last Colony in Africa: Diplomacy and the Independence of Rhodesia. Oxford: Basil Blackwell.

Chitagu, T.P. 2016. Framing of Zimbabwe's recurrent financial crisis in the post 2013 period: A case study of The Newsday and The Herald. Midlands State University. Unpublished MSc dissertation in Media and Society Studies.

Chitagu, T.P. 2018. The dangerous game: Relations between Zimbabwe's Independent Media and Zanu-PF. Reuters Institute Fellowship Paper, University of Oxford.

Chuma, W. 2003. The press, state and capital in the age of market failure and political turbulence: Zimbabwe, 1991-2003. Paper presented at the Conference on the Political Economy of the Media in Southern Africa, University of Natal.

Mano, W. 2005. Press freedom, professionalism and proprietorship: behind the Zimbabwean media divide. Westminster Papers in Communication and Culture (University of Westminster, London), Special Issue, October 2005: 56-70.

Mazango, E. 2005. Media games and shifting of spaces for political communication in Zimbabwe. Westminster Papers in Communication and Culture, Special Issue, November 2005: 33-55.

Media Monitoring Project of Zimbabwe (MMPZ), Media Alliance of Zimbabwe (MAZ) (2018), Reporting on Zimbabwe's Political Transition.

Media Professionalism and Ethics in Zimbabwe. 2002. A Report based on the Inquiry carried out by the Media Ethics Committee commissioned by the Department of Information and Publicity in the Office of the President and Cabinet of the Republic of Zimbabwe, February 2002.

MISA-Zimbabwe press statement 2 October 2009.

Mudzengi, E. 2009. Coordinator of the National Constitutional Assembly NGO, quoted in Zimbabwe Independent, 2 October 2009.

Mukasa, S. 2003. Press and politics in Zimbabwe. African Studies Quarterly, 7 (2 & 30) Fall 2003 http://www.africa.ufl.edu/asq/v7/v7i2-3a9.pdf

Phimister, I. 2004. Mugabe, Mbeki and the politics of anti-imperialism. Paper presented in Hannover: VAD Conference.

Randall, V. 1999. The media and democratisation in the Third World, Third World Quarterly 14(3): 624-646.

Ranger, T. 2004 Nationalist historiography, patriotic history and the history of the nation: The struggle over the past in Zimbabwe, Journal of Southern African Studies 30(2): 215-234.

Rønning, H. 2004. The media in Zimbabwe: The struggle between state and civil society' In: Darnolf, S. & Laakso, L. (eds). Twenty Years of Independence in Zimbabwe, Basingstoke and New York: Palgrave MacMillan.

Ronning, H. & Kupe, T. 2005. The dual legacy of democracy and authoritarianism: The media and the state in Zimbabwe. In: Curran, J. & Myung-Jin Park (eds). De-Westernising Media Studies, Routledge.

Sandbrook, R. 1996. Transitions without consolidation: Democratisation in six African cases. The Third World Quarterly, 17(1): 69-88.

Shelley, B. 2001. Protest and globalization: Media, symbols and audience in the drama of democratization, Democratization, 8(4): 155-174.

Sibanda, M. 2004. Complete control: Music and propaganda in Zimbabwe. In: Freedom of Musical Expression, 2004. http://freemuse.inforce.dk/sw7086.asp

Thram, D. 2006. Zvakwana-enough, 'media control and unofficial censorship of music in Zimbabwe'. In: Drewett, M. & Cloonan, M. (eds). Popular Music Censorship in Africa, Ashgate Publishing.

Waldahl, R. 2004. Politics and Persuasion: Media Coverage of Zimbabwe's 2000 Election. Harare: Weaver Press.

www.ingramcontent.com/pod-product-compliance
Lightning Source LLC
Chambersburg PA
CBHW081740270326
41932CB00020B/3346